D0815865

The
Resurrected
Jesus

Kwasi I. Kena

ABINGDON PRESS
Nashville

THE RESURRECTED JESUS

by Kwasi I. Kena

ISBN 0-687-09073-3

05 06 07 08 09 10—10 9 8 7 6 5 4 3 2

MANUFACTURED IN THE UNITED STATES OF AMERICA

Contents

Kwasi I. Kena currently serves with the General Board of Global Ministries of The United Methodist Church in Mission Personnel in New York. He and his wife Safiyah Fosua recently completed four years of missionary service in Ghana, West Africa.

Dr. Kena is a clergy member of the Iowa Annual Conference, where he served in pastoral ministry. He and Safiyah were the founding pastors of the Jubilee United Methodist Church in Waterloo, Iowa. Dr. Kena also enjoys teaching and writing. He has taught various courses in communication, social science, and religion at colleges and universities in Oklahoma and Iowa.

As a writer, Kwasi Kena's works have appeared in Cokesbury, Abingdon Press, Dimensions for Living, and Urban Ministries, Inc. publications. He is the author of *Forty Days in the Wilderness*, a devotional book for African American men and *In Plain View of the Cross*, a Lenten study. He also has contributed devotional material to *365 Meditations for Teens* and *365 Meditations for Families*.

A Word of Welcome

Welcome to *The Resurrected Jesus*, a study of the post-Resurrection appearances and the Ascension. *The Resurrected Jesus* picks up where *The Passion and Death of Jesus* leaves off—with Jesus' appearance to the disciples, his continued teaching, and the disciples' witness of his ascension to heaven. In this volume you will find

- narrative studies on the discovery of the empty tomb by Mary, the other women, the disciples, and the power of remembrance;
- the story of Jesus' appearance to the two travelers on the way to Emmaus and their joy in discovering who he was in the breaking of bread;
- Jesus' appearance to ten of the disciples as they gathered and hid in the days following the Crucifixion;
- Thomas's opportunity to see for himself the nail prints and other marks of crucifixion and Peter's transforming "reunion" with Jesus Christ, who forgave his denials and commissioned him to go to the "lost sheep";
- the story of Saul's conversion experience on the road to Damascus when his zeal was captured for the Lord;
- an explanation of resurrection through the lens of those who believed and those (the Sadducees) who did not;
- an exploration of the meaning of crucifixion and resurrection in Paul's letters;
- commentary on the Great Commission and the Ascension and their impact on disciples through the ages.

We invite you to delve deeply into this study of post-Resurrection stories and pray that you will find a blessing in it.

How to Use This Resource

We hope you enjoy participating in this study, either on your own or with a group. We offer these hints and suggestions to make your study a success.

The Resurrected Jesus is a self-contained study with all the teaching/learning suggestions conveniently located on or near the main text to which they refer. They are identified with the same heading (or a close abbreviation) as the heading in the main text. In addition to your Bible, all you need to have a successful group or individual study session is provided for you in this book.

Some special features are provided as well, such as the **Bible 301** activities in the teaching helps. We usually think of the "101" designation as the beginning level; these "301" designations prompt you to dig deeper. In these instances you will be invited to look up Scriptures, key words, or concepts in a Bible dictionary, commentary, or atlas. On occasion, an added book or resource is cited that may be obtained from your local library or perhaps from your pastor. Those resources are extras; your study will be enriched by these added sources of information, but it is not dependent on them.

This study is intentionally invitational. In the closing activity, you are invited to do three things: to give prayerful consideration to your relationship to Jesus Christ and make or renew your commitment, to offer your own spoken prayers, and to pray with and for others. We trust you will participate in these activities as you feel comfortable and that you will use them as a challenge to grow more confident in prayer and with your covenant with Jesus Christ.

Session One

What Does It Take for You to Believe?

Session Focus ■

Today's lesson invites us to explore the basis of our belief in the risen Savior and encourages us to answer the question, What does it take for you to believe?

Session Objective ■

This session will explore the process of arriving at faith in Christ. From the experience of the first witnesses of the risen Savior, we can learn about our own journey to faith.

Session Preparation ■

Have on hand a Bible concordance and hymnals.

Choose from among these activities and discussion starters to plan your lesson.

Seeing and Knowing ■

Read and compare the parallel accounts of today's passage and make a summary (Luke 24:1-12; Matthew 28:1-10; Mark 16:1-8; John 20:1-18). What did the witnesses see? What did they think they knew?

Luke 24:1-12

We've heard it a thousand times: "Is the glass half empty or half full?" If a psychologist showed you a blank sheet of paper, would you say it had nothing on it or that it was a space waiting to be filled with possibilities? Is life what we make it? Do we play a major role in determining our destiny? Does life lead us to crossroads that force us to choose between what we can see and what we can believe? What does it take for you to believe in something? People have mulled over these and similar questions for years, and these questions have a place in our spiritual and faith lives as well.

Seeing and Knowing

The "empty tomb" passages in each of the four Gospel accounts throw us into the fray of spiritual decision. Mary Magdalene and the other women witnesses say Jesus is not there. Mary says some men dressed in dazzling clothes told her that Jesus had risen from the dead. The initial response of the women and later of the disciples was not, "He is risen"; instead it was, "Where is the body?" It was more conceivable for them to believe that someone stole the body rather than to accept the fact that the Lord had risen from the dead.

Just a few days before, they had seen Jesus

What effect does fear or risk have on your willingness to recognize and trust in what God reveals? What is the effect of confusion or grief? of an attitude of acceptance and faith? What personal stories of risk and faith come to mind?

The Journey of Faith

Review Luke 24:1-12 again. Discuss the risks that the women witnesses initially faced in returning to the tomb. What did they actually encounter? (The Scripture does not mention the presence of the guards on Easter morning. What might have happened to them?)

Does your faith in Christ expose you to certain risks? Has your faith ever pushed you to act in ways that defy human logic and reason? Explain.

nailed to a cross, beaten, and suffering in agony. Just a few days before, Jesus had committed his spirit into God's hands and breathed his last breath. Just a few days before, one of the Roman soldiers pierced his side spilling water and blood from his body. Just a few days before, these women and Jesus' acquaintances watched the spectacle from a distance. Just a few days before, the women from Galilee went to the tomb and *saw* Jesus' body wrapped in linen burial cloth. They *knew* he was dead. As custom demanded, they then went to prepare special ointments and spices with which to anoint the body *after* they observed the sabbath on Saturday.

The Journey of Faith

Early Sunday morning, the women began a journey tinged with faith. They *knew* Jesus' body was in a sealed tomb (Luke 23:55). They undoubtedly knew that Roman soldiers guarded the tomb (Matthew 27:62-66). Nevertheless, they walked on toting spices and ointments with the intention of anointing Jesus' body. Logic and rational thinking may have considered the obstacles too prohibitive. People sometimes act in ways that defy human logic and reason, however. Individuals at times find the motivation to produce results that would be otherwise impossible. This action, this motivation, is called faith. "Who will roll the stone away from the entrance of the tomb?" (Mark 16:3, NIV). Inwardly, faith must have whispered, "I will."

Love, devotion, and gratitude also compelled this loyal group of women to travel to the tomb. Perhaps it is fitting that the Lord chose to reveal himself first to this group of women. They alone were willing to come in faith to perform the final burial customs. They alone were willing to risk confrontation with the Roman guards. They alone were compelled to extend their last expressions of love toward their fallen leader. Could it be that God, who is the rewarder of our faith, chose to reveal the risen Savior to them because of their faithful devotion? Whatever the reason, it should be an inspiration for us to make our own Sunday journeys of faith to meet the Lord in worship.

Bible 301 ☐

Using a concordance, look up the passages that mention Mary Magdalene. Draw a composite picture of her. What was she like? How would you describe her relationship with Jesus? How does what you have traditionally heard about her compare with the Scripture? In what ways, if any, can you relate to her or her experiences?

What do you think motivated Mary Magdalene in particular to risk returning to the tomb? We often say we owe God a debt of gratitude. How would you pay such a debt?

Mary Magdalene and Jesus

Mary Magdalene had particular reason to attend to Jesus one final time. From her, Scripture reports, Jesus had cast out seven demons (Luke 8:2). The mention of the number seven indicates an unusually large number of demonic spirits in residence. After experiencing such a magnificent deliverance, we can only imagine the immense gratitude and devotion that Mary had toward the Lord. Jesus commented on the kind of extravagant love that Mary Magdalene was capable of when he was anointed by a sinful woman while he was at table.

At Nain, according to Luke's Gospel, Jesus told a parable of two men unable to pay their debts to a moneylender. One owed a great sum and the other, a smaller sum. Seeing their inability to pay, the moneylender then canceled both debts. "Now which of them will love him more?" Jesus asked. The answer, of course, is the one who had the bigger debt (Luke 7:40-43).

Just as Jesus had released the sinful woman from her debt of sin, he had also released Mary Magdalene from tremendous spiritual captivity. She could do nothing less than lavish

Jesus with her love and devotion. Mary Magdalene was foremost among honorable women of substance who supported Jesus' ministry (Luke 8:1-3). If for no other reason, she had just cause to pay her final respects to the man who had tremendously blessed her so.

Like Mary Magdalene, we too owe a debt of gratitude to Christ for paying the price of our sin on the cross. We too may not fully understand all that we have heard or read about the Lord. Still, we can come to express our love and gratitude to Christ through worship.

We may need to consider our motivations for becoming a Christian and following the Lord. Does our Christianity depend on compelling faith or cold facts? Do we follow the Lord based on unequivocal proofs or an inward witness of God's Spirit? The empty tomb confronted the women witnesses and the eleven disciples with the challenge of believing whether Jesus had risen from the dead. What would it take for them to believe? What does it take for us to believe? This tenacious question will accompany us throughout this chapter, urging us to arrive at some personal resolution.

The Powerful Effect of Remembering

The Powerful Effect of Remembering
Read Luke 26:6-8 and John 14:25-26. What is the importance of memory? What is the difference between remembering, as promised by Jesus through the Holy Spirit, and reminiscing?

In Luke's account, the two men in dazzling clothes had to refocus the women's attention on Jesus' word about his crucifixion and resurrection. "Remember how he told you, while he was still in Galilee: 'The Son of Man must be delivered into the hands of sinful men, be crucified and on the third day be raised again.' *Then they remembered his words*" (Luke 24:6-8, NIV, italics added).

Have each of three small groups look up a different one of these passages: Matthew 17:22-23; Mark 9:30-31; Luke 9:43b-45. Which of Jesus' words are the most important? What do you think he would have wanted his disciples to be able to recall quickly and clearly?

Bible 301 ☐

Look up your favorite hymns. How do the lyrics (or the music) prompt you to recall various elements and tenets of the faith? For some persons, the musical setting evokes stronger memories and responses to God than reciting Scripture, for example. How do these hymns act as a memory aid for you?

Take turns telling *brief* stories (no more than two minutes each) about family, a personal special moment, a turning point in life, or another subject of the storyteller's choosing. Notice what the storyteller thought was important to include and what details were missing. How can you begin to identify the values that underlie the story? Next, take turns retelling the Easter story and do the same observation and analysis. How does the way the events are remembered and retold reflect the importance and values of the teller? How does that telling serve to enhance and maintain faith? How

In Matthew, Mark, and Luke, Jesus mentioned his betrayal, crucifixion, and resurrection to "his disciples" while he was in Galilee (Matthew 17:22-23; Mark 9:30; Luke 9:43b-45). Mark's account specifically mentions that in Galilee, Jesus held a private audience with his disciples and predicted his death and resurrection (Mark 9:30-31). Were the women numbered among the Lord's disciples? The men in dazzling clothes jogged the women's memories to recall a specific conversation that Jesus had with them in Galilee. Somewhere, sometime, in Galilee, the women heard directly from the Lord.

What happens when we remember? When we look at our family photo albums, we remember and relive the events captured on film. Emotions return, smiles flash, and interest rekindles as we recall those memories. Before long, we begin talking about what happened. The excitement of the moment consumes a room full of relatives. Soon everyone is transported back to the time when "Uncle Felix accidentally swallowed his false teeth." In certain African cultures, a person remains "alive" as long as he or she is remembered—through recounting a story about them, mentioning their names on special occasions. Our Christian faith lives as we remember what Christ did for us on Calvary's cross. Telling and retelling "the old, old story" is vital to our spiritual growth.

In today's passage, the two men at the empty tomb asked the women to remember what Jesus had told them in Galilee (Luke 24:6). Unfortunately, we do not have the luxury of sitting in the physical presence of Jesus and hearing the actual sound of his voice. We do, however, have the Scriptures to read and internalize. Except for Christ's incarnation, Scripture remains as one of

do stories keep persons, including Jesus Christ, "alive" and vital for our own lives?

Have you ever felt that the Holy Spirit helped bring to remembrance something vital to you at a crucial time? How would you describe that experience and the effect it had on the situation at the time?

What barriers have prevented you from being able to think or act faithfully (or theologically) at a crucial time? What would it take to overcome these barriers? What are potential sources of help?

The Bible in My Head

Were you taught to memorize Bible verses? If so, what is your favorite? Why? Do you think it is a valid and effective activity for children? Explain. Did you enjoy the activity at the time? Do you now work to remember at least the import of particular passages, if not the exact wording? If so, what motivates you? What personal benefits do you gain from studying and remembering Scripture?

Why do you think the women witnesses were motivated to remember Jesus' predictions? How do you see the women

God's most personal vehicles for communication with us. Have you discovered the value of committing Scripture to memory?

Getting the Bible in My Head

Consider the following illustration from Ministry in an Oral Culture: Living with Will Rogers, Uncle Remus, and Minnie Pearl, *by Tex Sample (Westminster/John Knox Press, 1994). A pastor fresh from seminary education thought he would introduce a more contemporary way of teaching Scripture. "We're going to do away with Bible memorization for children," he announced with bold naivete. "Instead," he pronounced knowing that he echoed the sentiments of leading experts, "we're simply going to explain what the Scriptures mean."*

"We're not going to do that," retorted one of the matriarchs of the church. She went on to explain why she refused to agree with her pastor: It seems that the children in that area consistently dropped out of Sunday school by age sixteen. After high school they went off to work, to get married and have children of their own. She hoped that as they began to raise their children, they would eventually return to church. In the meantime, she reasoned knowingly, the only Bible they will have is the one in their heads. "That's why we are going to teach them to memorize Bible verses. If it's in there [in their minds and memories], someday they may come back to the church because they learned early how important faith is."

The women at the empty tomb recalled the words that Jesus had spoken to them in Galilee. In light of Jesus' missing body and the charge of the two men to remember Jesus' prediction of his resurrection, the women had just cause to wipe the dust from

attempting to make sense out of these events? What evidence indicates that people use Scripture to help them make sense out of life events? How relevant have you found Scripture to be in guiding you through puzzling events in life? Explain.

their memories. Mere knowledge of what Jesus had said was not enough, though.

The women not only were encouraged to *remember* Jesus' words, these new circumstances now motivated them to take a closer look at the *meaning* of his words. They had to reach deep inside and infuse those dormant words with life. They had to see the relevance of Christ's words to their present situation. In short, they had to attach their faith to God's Word in order for it to make sense and come alive to them. Now, they had to act on their belief in Jesus' word. So, in faith and action, these women disciples of Christ set out to tell the rest of the disciples all that had happened.

The Package of Reality

The Package of Reality ◼

Imagine that you have been asked to explain the Resurrection (which you have "seen" yourself through the Bible and through your faith experiences) to someone who understands at least the basics of the Hebrew Scriptures. What would you say? Form pairs and try to explain the event to your partner.

Now imagine that your listener has considered your eyewitness account as an idle tale. How do you feel? respond?

Read John 20:1-18. How did Peter and John respond to the news of the Resurrection? How did what they witnessed differ from what the women saw and what difference did that make in how the men accepted the truth?

The report of the women threw all of the disciples into a quandary. They struggled to determine whether the report was real or absurd. The women witnesses were hardly taken seriously at first. To the apostles it seemed to be an "idle tale," and they did not believe the women (Luke 24:1-11). In response to this "idle tale," John's Gospel records that Peter and the disciple "whom Jesus loved" (probably John) raced to the tomb. Upon entering the tomb and verifying that Jesus was not there, John believed (John 20:2-8).

But, what did he believe? The next verse says, "for as yet they did not understand the scripture, that he must rise from the dead" (John 20:9). The disciples searched for and found an answer that they could conceptualize—Jesus' body was missing. They still struggled to believe the unbelievable—that Jesus had risen from the dead. What is credible truth for us? Whom do we trust to bring us reliable information?

Truth in Packaging ▪

What three "packages" does Tex Sample mention and which is the most compelling source of information for you? What is the most compelling source of truth for you regarding theological and faith issues? (For example: As a visual person, I may be drawn to the visual media as a preferred way to receive information, but I wouldn't watch a movie about Jesus as a trustworthy theological source. I would read my Bible, a literate "package." Other persons may watch a favorite evangelist on television and listen to the Bible reading and sermon, an oral "package.")

Have you ever been asked to believe in something that you thought was contrary to fact? Whom do you trust to bring you reliable information?

What would it take to convince you to trust in something controversial?

How well are you able to accept the "packaging of reality" of Scripture as expressed by the oral culture of biblical peoples?

Are proofs and facts relevant in building your faith in Christ? Can undeniable proofs and facts adequately explain the resurrection of Jesus Christ? Explain.

"Truth in Packaging"

According to Tex Sample, a specialist in the study of blue-collar workers and poor people, the social landscape of the United States is made up of three types of people. Each group looks for truth, authenticity, and validity in distinctively different "packages." One group relates to the multimedia world of sound, light, and movement. Their source of multisensory information comes largely from video, audio, or electronic media. Other people fall into the "literate" category. This refers to the world of written discourse. Here, academic critique, finely honed definitions, thoroughly documented arguments, and well-respected experts attract attention. Finally, there is the oral culture. For this group, stories and proverbs, memory and relationship, experience and practicality rule the day. What package must reality wear in order to gain your attention and respect?

The fabric of biblical peoples is woven with the hand-spun threads of oral culture. In oral cultures, people understand things through stories, proverbs, and relationships. A man raised in oral culture remarked, "We often knew a lot that we could not put into words (because we didn't *have* the right words) but that we nevertheless knew how to *do*. We knew things we couldn't say, we felt things we couldn't name, and we did things we couldn't explain" (*Ministry in an Oral Culture: Living with Will Rogers, Uncle Remus, & Minnie Pearl*, by Tex Sample).

Since the Bible is the written account of an oral people, its "packaging of reality" may not satisfy other types of people. If we prefer tons of solid facts and verifiable historical

The Jews constantly told the stories of their spiritual journey as a people. How does your family record and express its spiritual journey?

data about the events surrounding Jesus' resurrection, the Bible will sorely disappoint us. Oral cultures have not and will not pack reality inside of "literate" packages. That means that in order to meet Jesus as Resurrected Christ, we may need to re-examine the demands that we make of Scripture.

The women saw and heard from the angelic visitors to the empty tomb. They ran to tell others, all means of knowing and communicating in an oral culture. Eyewitnesses played a vital role in the legal system of this culture. "A single witness shall not suffice to convict a person of any crime or wrongdoing in connection with any offense that may be committed. Only on the evidence of two or three witnesses shall a charge be sustained" (Deuteronomy 19:15). One person could be mistaken or terribly biased in a situation; but with two or three witnesses to an event, surely thorough inquiry would lead to the truth.

According to the traditions of the day, one would think that the disciples would have believed this *group* of women witnesses; they were among Jesus' intimate friends and companions. Would these women, well-known and continuing members of the inner circle, fabricate a story about an empty tomb and men in dazzling clothes? At the very least, we should expect the disciples to ask these women a few questions. That might have been the case—if the witnesses at the empty tomb had been men.

Women and Witnesses

For what possible reasons did the disciples fail to believe the report of the women witnesses? Recall

Women and Witnesses

The fortunes and status of women throughout the biblical centuries changed and evolved. During the second Temple period (from about the mid-sixth century until a generation before

your exercise in imagining that you tried to tell your own eyewitness account. Now imagine that someone you know well heard your story and didn't immediately believe you. How would you feel? What would you do? How might you get beyond the barrier of familiarity?

the birth of Jesus), women were not considered credible witnesses and were not to be seen in public or to speak to strangers. Women were generally relegated to the private space of their households to tend to domestic duties. Women alone were not regarded as worthy of spiritual instruction. When they did participate in synagogue activities, they were segregated from the men. Obviously these practices were not always followed stringently and they did change, or Mary and the other women would not have been allowed to associate with Jesus so freely. They were doubtless affected by the general social rules of that day.

From Amazement to Belief

How would you describe Peter's spiritual condition at the close of Luke 24:1-12? Review the quote about the mature believer. Is he describing Peter? you? Explain.

Moving From Amazement Toward Belief

So many obstacles hinder our understanding of Jesus the risen Christ. Our own limited ability to comprehend spiritual matters causes us to gaze erroneously at the concrete world for spiritual insights. We, like Peter and John, may have rushed to verify that the tomb was empty and the body missing without considering that the Lord had actually risen from the dead. We too may hesitate to accept spiritual truths because we do not trust the messenger's gender or culture or ethnicity. As long as we remain overly concerned about the "package" of reality, we remain in danger of missing God's truth altogether. Somehow, we must learn to recognize the message of God's truth regardless of the outside "packaging." God has the ability to share the truth with us in ways that our human spirit can recognize.

Today's passage concludes with the picture of Peter at home wondering about what had just happened. One biblical scholar claims that, "The mature believer does not accept belief in God tentatively, hypothetically, or until something better comes along. . . . The mature [believer] commits himself to belief in God . . . he accepts belief in God as basic" ("Is Belief in God Rational?" in *Rationality and Religious Belief*, edited by C. F. Delaney, University of Notre Dame Press, 1979). While there is no doubt that Peter believed in God, we cannot say that he was a mature believer in Christ's resurrection at this point.

Clinging to Hope

We can safely believe that Peter was at least *hoping* that Jesus had risen from the dead. As a man from an oral culture, Peter may have been at the brink of knowing things about God that he *could not put into words*. He may have been *feeling things he couldn't name*. He may have begun to *do things he couldn't explain*. Those are characteristics of having a living relationship with the risen Christ. Initially, though, Peter was still moving toward fully experiencing God. He was on the threshold of faith, hoping Christ had risen from the dead.

One of the endearing features of hope is that it provides comfort. Hope does not always require *probability*; it just requires that we believe that what we are hoping for is *possible* (even if it isn't). There is hope for us here. We too can begin our journey with the resurrected Savior even if our first step begins in hope. If we just believe that there is the possibility that Jesus was crucified, died, and raised from the dead, we'll find strength to continue walking. But, as we amble toward a surer faith in the risen Savior, we, like Peter and the other disciples, may encounter doubts.

Despair has been described as a type of

Clinging to Hope ■

Identify four or five events, including the Resurrection, that we would consider miraculous or that would require extraordinary circumstances to achieve a desired outcome. (For example, a loved one is seriously injured and has a 3 percent chance of living, or you want to buy a house but your earnings are too low or your debt too high to obtain financing.)

Now do a forced choice exercise. Identify a place to indicate "high hopes" and another to indicate "deep despair." Read aloud the events in turn, assuming that they involve you. Move to the place on the continuum that indicates your level of hope. (For example, if my loved one were injured, how hopeful would I be of that 3 percent chance of recovery occurring?) Where have you located yourself and why?

If you were one of the initial disciples, how hopeful do you think you might have been that Jesus really was not dead but resurrected and alive? (Stand in that location and explain.)

Compare how others perceive their level of hopefulness in the variety of events. What helps to sustain hope and belief? What are some of the benefits of hope? How can hope help us along our spiritual journey toward belief?

Close With Devotions

Spend a few minutes in silence thinking about or writing in a journal about what it takes for you truly to believe in the Resurrection and all that it means for your life and faith.

Receive prayer requests. Invite especially prayers that deal with belief, hope, despair, and doubt. Then close with this prayer:

Lord, we confess that your ways are often beyond our understanding. Like the early disciples, we need to be reminded to recall the meaning of Scripture. Help us to trust you despite the threat of personal harm. Help us to bear witness to Christ even if it puts our reputations at peril. Cast out doubt, fear, despair, and unbelief; and bring to mind the great story of our faith. May we always be your trusted witnesses; in Jesus' name. Amen.

pain experienced when hope is gone or all but lost. Peter believed Jesus was dead. He believed Jesus was gone forever. Yet, this new evidence prodded him to consider a new "packaging" of reality. What does it take for us to believe new things? Peter may have experienced doubt and despair, but he also had hope.

There is no magic formula for believing in Christ the Risen Savior. It may take a different experience for each of us to be convinced that Christ lived, died, and was raised from the dead for our salvation. Once we are convinced however, we will find that our Christian beliefs serve as "action guides" for us. If Peter were to believe that Jesus had indeed risen from the dead at this point in the passage, we would expect him to act differently—wouldn't we? No longer would he grieve over the apparent loss of Jesus. Instead, he would be asking questions like, Now what and where do we go from here, Lord?

We end this chapter where we began by asking, What does it take for us to believe in the Resurrection? Life places us at spiritual crossroads. Do we have hope? God speaks to us through the Scriptures. Can we accept biblical truth in whatever forms that God chooses to "package" it? How can we recognize how the Lord has already sent us a living witness of his love, grace, and mercy. God can provide whatever it takes for us to believe.

Session Two

The Revelation of the Risen Christ

Session Focus ■

This lesson focuses on Christ's determined effort to reveal himself to his disciples through his physical appearances, recalling the Scriptures, and sharing a simple meal.

Session Objective ■

As we study the process by which Christ revealed himself to first-century disciples, we should reflect on the ways in which Christ continues to reveal himself to twenty-first century disciples.

Session Preparation ■

Have on hand a Bible concordance, a Bible commentary, and a Bible dictionary.

Choose from among these activities and discussion starters to plan your lesson.

Luke 24:13-49; John 20:19-2

"I just can't believe it!" We frequently utter these words when we learn of the unexpected death of a loved one. Ironically, Jesus' disciples struggled with these thoughts after learning about the unexpected *life* of a loved one—the risen Christ. They simply could not believe that Jesus was alive.

As we pick up the action in verse 13, Luke focuses his historical lens on two disciples walking toward a village named Emmaus. Cleopas and his unnamed companion were abuzz about the startling "rumors" that began circulating about Jesus that Sunday morning. Despite these spectacular "rumors," the two travelers journeyed toward Emmaus laden with despair and uncertainty. Even the literal appearance of the risen Christ did not initially snap them out of their melancholy mood. Something prevented them from recognizing the risen Savior. Jesus found them as he finds us at various times—oblivious to him.

Later, Jesus found the Eleven in Jerusalem wondering whether he was truly alive. Both in Emmaus and in Jerusalem, Jesus appeared to his disciples to persuade them that he indeed had risen. Painstakingly, Christ reminded them of what Scripture says about his resurrection. Lovingly, he broke bread with them. Then the Lord opened their minds to understand what the Scriptures said about him. In Jerusalem, he breathed on them, and they received the Holy Spirit. This was an historic moment—the birthing of the church.

First Steps With the Risen Savior

Learning to walk with the risen Savior is not unlike a baby taking his first steps. "Be afraid, Jaereth is beginning to walk," came the playful e-mail message about our only grandchild. After weeks of scooting and crawling around the floor, little Jaereth decided it was time to start doing what big people do. Under the watchful eyes of his proud parents, Jaereth searched for reliable, sturdy objects to grab for support. He needed something trustworthy to hold onto while he steadied his wobbly legs. Secure with his support, Jaereth was braced and ready to take his first shaky steps.

Our first steps with Christ are sometimes uncertain. As we begin our spiritual journeys, we often clutch the familiar hoping that it will aid our walk into the unknown. As Jesus joined the two travelers to Emmaus, they needed some familiar handle to grasp. How else would they be able to reconcile the unfathomable idea that Christ actually had been raised from the dead?

Perhaps so as not to shock them, Jesus wisely opted to ease his way into their company. "What are you discussing together as you walk along?" he asked (Luke 24:17, NIV). They stopped short, sadness written across their faces. We can take comfort in knowing that Jesus understands how an erratic emotional state can dull our spiritual perception.

Many of us know how distress can paralyze our capacity to think, believe, and act.

First Steps With the Savior

Read Luke 24:13-21. Cleopas and his companion were not expecting to see Jesus; he was dead, after all. Have you ever realized in retrospect that God had somehow touched your life when you didn't expect it?

How would you characterize your relationship with Jesus Christ? If you are fairly new to it or if the means of communion (such as prayer, Bible reading, and so on) are new or difficult for you, you may not immediately recognize when something godly is working in your life. (This is OK; it takes practice!)

How did Jesus include himself in these disciples' presence? In what simple ways might Jesus Christ be trying to include himself in your life? Are there things that prevent you from recognizing God's activity in your life? Explain.

Read Luke 24:22-35. The disciples had hoped that Jesus would redeem Israel from the oppressive Roman government. In what areas do you see the need for redemption? Where do you hope to see the redemption of the Lord in this country?

What areas of your life are most in need of redemption and renewal?

The two disciples finally recognized Jesus at the meal. In what daily activities is the sense of the divine most obvious and accessible to you? the least obvious?

One commentator suggests that these emotionally distraught disciples were suffering from depression. Depression commonly sets in when we believe that the world has yanked the rug out from under us. Could that be what the two disciples were experiencing?

The Crucifixion was a terrifying spectacle that severed them from the Lord. They felt they had lost everything that mattered to them. They had made emotional investments, hoping and dreaming about a promising future with the Messiah in a newly restored Israel. Imagine the faraway look in their eyes when they said, "We had hoped that he was the one to redeem Israel" (Luke 24:21a).

Before their shaken faith could recognize the resurrected Lord, Jesus Christ would have to dispel their fears. Their aborted hopes needed to be resurrected. They needed a sturdy handle to grasp as they took their first tentative steps with Christ.

Scripture: A Familiar Anchor

A significant part of Hebrew tradition and education centered in learning the Scriptures, for them what we call the Old Testament or the Hebrew Scriptures. Boys were taught to read so that they could read the Torah, which was the heart of the community.

What is the heart of your community? What are the familiar anchors that hold your life in place? What part does God play in that heart of life? What part do the Scriptures play?

Scripture: A Familiar Anchor

Though Jesus walked beside them, the disciples remained oblivious to his identity. As far as they were concerned, their last vestige of hope had perished because it was now the third day since Jesus had died. According to Jewish belief, a person's spirit hovered about its corpse for three days. After the third day however, any hopes of the person returning to life were dashed.

You would think that the appearance of the risen Christ would cure the disciples' spiritual myopia. In so many ways, however, we are like they were, needing some familiar anchor to steady our uncertainties. As Jesus had done so often in his earthly ministry, he provided a reliable handle for the disciples to grasp—Scripture.

Jesus called the two disciples "foolish" (Luke 24:25). Why? What "spiritual myopia" plagues you?

"Then he said to them, 'Oh, how foolish you are, and how slow of heart to believe all that the prophets have declared! Was it not necessary that the Messiah should suffer these things and then enter into his glory?' " (Luke 24:25-26). Jesus' sharp words redirected their gaze away from woeful despair to the promise of Scripture. Jesus' use of the word *foolish* refers to their thoughtless and dull understanding of what the Scriptures say about Messiah. Although the disciples were already familiar with the Scriptures, their previous opinions and prejudices clouded their understanding. They could not see the scriptural evidence that Jesus must die and rise from the dead. We often suffer from the same spiritual malady today.

Bible 301 ☐

Using the technique that Morely describes, take turns identifying Scripture verses (or things you hold to be true in faith) and tell what they mean to you and why they are important, even transformational.

Look up the Bible verses. Using a concordance and a Bible commentary, locate the verses. Dig deeper into the context, the history, the relevance of the passage for its original hearers. Knowing these facts, how is the passage enhanced for you? What further impact or importance does it have for your own faith formation?

Hearing God in the Scriptures

Patrick Morely, author of The Seven Seasons of a Man's Life *(Zondervan, 1997), remarked that early in his spiritual pilgrimage, he taught Bible study groups in which the participants merely shared their opinions. "We sat around in a circle, and each told the others what a verse of the Bible meant to him. It never dawned on me that we should be asking each other, 'What does it mean to God?' " Shouldn't Bible study be more than accumulating and redistributing our opinions about God?*

Simple familiarity with the Bible and factual knowledge of Scripture is not enough to reveal the Savior to us. Bible teachers constantly stress the difference between "knowing about God" and "knowing God." The emphasis in many Bible study groups now is on transformation. In transformational Bible study, the aim is to encounter the living God

Describe the difference between transformational Bible study and the kind of Bible study that Patrick Morely taught in the illustration. How is this study, for example, leading you to reflect on the Scriptures and the way God intervenes and calls you in life?

Would you say that you are better at knowing God or knowing *about* God? Are you satisfied with your way of knowing? Do you want to know more or know better? How can you accomplish this knowing?

through the Scripture. In such encounters, we give God an open invitation to communicate Scripture to us. In transformational Bible study, we allow the Word to shape us.

"Beginning with Moses and all the prophets" (meaning their own Scriptures), Jesus invited the disciples to "encounter" him as risen Christ. Masterfully, Jesus rehearsed everything that the Scriptures say concerning him. These Scriptures provided all the evidence the disciples needed to understand that Messiah must suffer the passion of the cross in order to glory in the Resurrection. For these Jewish disciples, the Law and the Prophets were familiar anchors.

When Words Are Not Enough ■

Share your reactions to the notion that it takes multiple encounters with Christ before a person gives his or her life to the Lord. Name the most effective ways in which you encounter Christ.

Form five small groups and assign to each group one of the senses—taste, touch, sight, feel, and hearing. Take at least three or four minutes to identify as many ways as you can of sensing the work and presence of Christ using that particular sense. (For example, how can you taste the presence? in Communion elements? in a meal served to the homeless? and so on.)

When Words Are Not Enough

At times, it is difficult to read the Bible without becoming judgmental. Jesus literally walked with these disciples and gave them a private Bible study about himself! With 20/20 hindsight, we may lose patience with these disciples and ask, "What more did they need?" In reality, we earthbound creatures commonly need considerable convincing before we fully trust Christ. Christian conversion is a process.

In seminary, I recall hearing that it takes twenty-one separate "witnessing experiences" or "encounters with Christ" before a person surrenders his or her life to the Lord. To me, that means we need a variety of encounters with the Lord. There is no *single* way to convince our souls to embrace the risen Christ as our personal Lord and Savior. The disciples needed more than words. They needed to see and touch the risen Savior. They needed to hear him teach the sacred words of

Together, compare your lists. What new insights arise? How are your senses heightened to experience the presence of Christ and the work of the Holy Spirit?

Considering the brainstormed list of sensory avenues to Christ, imagine your worship service incorporating three or four of these avenues. How would the worship experience change? Would these changes be an improvement? a distraction? a blessing?

A Simple Meal With Christ ■

In the intimacy of a simple meal, the two disciples recognized Christ (Luke 24:30-31). How could you use mealtime to remember Christ and practice your Christian faith?

Is sharing the Lord's Supper a meaningful way for you to experience the risen Christ? In your experience, how important has the act of sharing a meal with others promoted the spread of Christian love and fellowship?

Scriptures. They needed to taste and smell the bread he served. They needed the help of the Holy Spirit to reveal the resurrected Christ to them.

Like the two disciples, we also need a variety of creative ways of experiencing the reality of the risen Lord. Words alone may not convince some of us to believe in Christ. We may need to involve all our senses in worship. We may need more transformational Bible study. We may need to offer the Lord's Supper more frequently. We may need to include more drama and visual arts. We may need more solitude and silent meditation or more vigorous music and exuberant dance. Each opportunity we present carries the potential to open a door to understanding the risen Savior.

After the Lord carefully explained the Scriptures, however, the disciples still did not understand. As we are about to see, Jesus' loving disciples needed something else—communion with the Lord.

A Simple Meal With Christ

Night was about to descend on that first Easter Sunday, as Jesus and the two disciples neared Emmaus. Jesus acted as if he were going farther, but the disciples urged him to stay and eat with them. They offered him hospitality, a cultural kindness that would yield spiritual enlightenment.

After serving as a missionary in Ghana, West Africa, I have a greater appreciation for the crucial importance of hospitality. In many ways, Ghanaian culture parallels Old Testament culture. If you happen upon a Ghanaian who is eating, he or she invariably smiles, acknowledges your presence, and invites you to share the meal. That gesture of hospitality is quite significant because food is a precious commodity. Ghana is the

Invite stories of intercultural hospitality from anyone who has traveled to another country or has spent time with a cultural group different from your own.

Bible 301 ☐

Using a Bible dictionary, look up hospitality and some of the Bible references that illuminate how hospitality was offered (or not) in Bible times. What did it mean to be a good host? a good guest? What are some examples of a breach of etiquette by either guest or host? What are the consequences of those failures? Note how the demonstration of hospitality turned a stranger into a friend. How are the values that undergird and illustrate biblical hospitality like your own sense of hospitality? How are they different?

Have you sensed Christ's presence during a time in which you gave or received hospitality? Tell about that experience.

tenth poorest country on a continent of more than fifty countries. Still, even as a stranger, you are humbly invited to dip your hand into your host's bowl to eat. Although the disciples did not recognize Jesus, they invited him to dip his hand into their bowl.

Communion, simply defined, is fellowship with God. It occurs between Christ and his people. It happens under the direction of the Holy Spirit. It takes place among believers. We refer to the Lord's Supper as Communion because in it there is fellowship between Christ and his disciples. While scholars point out that the meal shared by Jesus and the two disciples was not the sacrament, Luke's inclusion of the meal should cause us to consider the spiritual significance of meals and intimate fellowship with Christ.

As the Lord performed the familiar acts of taking, blessing, breaking, and giving the bread, the disciples finally realized who was dining with them. There is an element of trust and intimacy achieved at mealtime.

The obvious spiritual connection between meals and the risen Christ comes through the sharing of the Lord's Supper. Something revelatory happens when we gather at the Lord's Table to partake of the body and blood of Christ. The mystery of Christ's resurrection is communicated through this sacrament in ways that do not occur anywhere else in worship. As we gather, the words of institution turn our hearts and minds back to the cross to consider thoughtfully what Christ has done for us. Paul reminds us that each time we "eat this bread and drink the cup [we] proclaim the Lord's death until he comes" (1 Corinthians 11:26). Through Christ's death the penalty for our sins is paid. Through Christ's resurrection, the Lord has made forgiveness of sins and eternal life possible.

There are other meals that carry spiritual significance. John Wesley promoted the love feast, which encouraged fellowship among the saints. Christian love is not a private matter; it is to be shared. As we learn to share God's love in the nonthreatening setting of a meal, we can encourage others to seek fellowship with the Lord and the body of Christ.

Peace Be With You!

Peace Be With You!

Read Luke 24:36-43 and John 20:19-21. This, for both Luke and John, is the second post-Resurrection appearance of Jesus Christ, although the two are different. Compare them. How are they different? similar?

How did Christ address the fears of his disciples? What means did he use to reassure the disciples that they could trust what they were seeing? How do you imagine you would have felt if you had seen someone you loved dearly but knew to be dead? Could you have touched Jesus' wounds? Would you feel peaceful in this circumstance? Explain.

Bible 301 ☐

What are some of the striking features of Christ's peace? Read Mark 4:39, 5:34; Luke 10:6; John 16:33; and enough of the surrounding verses to understand the context. Have you ever had the sense of Christ's peace to surround you? If so, what was the circumstance and how did you feel about it?

In John 20:19-23, Jesus appeared in Jerusalem amid a lively discussion among his disciples. Luke tells us that the Emmaus Road disciples, to whom Jesus had revealed himself earlier, had returned to Jerusalem. If we join the two accounts, it would appear that they were already with the other disciples, telling their story. It was evening, according to both Luke and John, and the disciples were behind locked doors, afraid of the Jews (John 20:19).

While they were excitedly discussing the latest news, Jesus approached them saying, "Peace be with you" (John 20:19). Christ immediately addressed the disciples' fear with this greeting that was a wish of peace and prosperity for body and soul. After their initial joyful reaction, he repeated his greeting (20:21). This peace offered every earthly and heavenly good to them. There is a striking parallel between this salutation, the one in Luke 24:36, and Jesus' kind address to the disciples in John 14.

In John 14, Jesus realized the approaching hour of his crucifixion. Carefully, he explained to the disciples why he was about to leave them. Before he finished, he gave them divine encouragement. He promised that he would return and that he would send the Holy Spirit to comfort and teach them. Finally, he gave them his peace. "Peace I leave with you; my peace I give you. . . . Do

If you told someone else, what was the reaction?

Read John 14:25-31. Jesus had tried to prepare the disciples for this post-Resurrection visit. Did it work? Do you think that would have been sufficient to prepare you? Explain.

Receive the Holy Spirit
Read John 20:22-23.

Jesus gives to us, as a part of the faith community, the responsibility to extend his ministry against sin by proclaiming the truth of Christ. For this work, we are empowered by the Holy Spirit.

What does all this mean to you? Taking this mandate seriously, would your life have to change? your beliefs? your theological understanding and sophistication? Are you willing to make any changes to fulfill this mandate? Explain.

We can interpret this teaching on forgiveness on two levels, as is typical with John's Gospel. One is the forgiveness just discussed—the extension of Jesus' ministry against sin. The other is the personal forgiveness we are all called to practice against the insults of daily life.

Form small groups of two or three and share with one another how high you perceive your "forgiveness quotient" to be. Is forgiveness

not let your hearts be troubled and do not be afraid" (John 14:27, NIV). It is more than coincidence that the risen Savior begins his conversation with the startled disciples in Jerusalem by reacquainting them with the peace he had given them earlier.

Receive the Holy Spirit

John's Gospel account also includes the details of what is known as the "Johannine Pentecost." Traditionally, the Day of Pentecost in Acts 2 is regarded as the "birthday" of the church. If we understand the church to be a body of people who believe in the risen Christ through the power of the Holy Spirit, then the church was actually "born" on Easter Sunday evening. Through this encounter with Jesus, the disciples came to believe in the resurrected Christ. Jesus then breathed on them, bestowing the Holy Spirit. Through this act, Jesus empowered the faith community with the authority to carry out his next command—to forgive or retain peoples' sins (John 20:21-23).

The New Interpreter's Bible (Vol. IX, Abingdon Press, 1995) makes three crucial points about John 20:22-23. First, Jesus' words in verse 23 are addressed to the entire faith community. Second, the disciples' ability to forgive or not is understood in the context of their being sent (verse 21) with the power of the Holy Spirit (verse 22) and not with their own judgment or concept of personal authority. Third, as an extension of Jesus' ministry, the community must interpret Jesus' actions and teaching regarding sin, which for John is a theological failure, not a moral or behavioral one.

Clearly, the ultimate authority to forgive sins belongs to God, and this authority was demonstrated many times by Jesus. John's

easy for you? Do you hang on to things that ought to be let go? Do you expect to be excused or forgiven in circumstances that you do not accord to others? How can the Holy Spirit help you to release yourself from bondage to unforgiveness?

Close With Prayer ■

Receive prayer requests. After praying for special concerns, join together in the following prayer:

Dear Lord, we stand amazed by the many ways that you reveal yourself to us. Throughout the upcoming week, reveal yourself to us in new refreshing ways. Prepare our hearts to serve you as faithful Christian witnesses. Grant us the courage to forgive others when we do not want to forgive. Give us the enthusiasm to share the good news of Christ at your direction.

Gospel introduces this theme early, when, for example, John the Baptist addressed Jesus as "the Lamb of God who takes away the sin of the world" (John 1:29). Sin, which brings about death, can be overcome through belief in Christ. Later, Jesus drew a contrast between death and belief: "If you do not believe that I am the one I claim to be, you will indeed die in your sins" (John 8:24b, NIV).

As the risen Savior, who has just overcome sin and death, Jesus is giving the disciples and the whole faith community the authority to continue his mission on earth.

The Lord worked diligently to establish belief in him as the resurrected Lord within his disciples. Through bodily appearances, sharing Scripture, and breaking bread, the risen Lord revealed himself to his trusted followers. Establishing personal belief in Christ is not the only goal of Christianity, however. Christ reveals himself to us so that we may share his revelation with others.

Session Three

Clearing Away Uncertainties

Session Focus ■

This session focuses on doubt, estrangement, and our relationship with Jesus Christ.

Session Objective ■

Our goal in this session is to explore the determined manner in which Christ establishes faith and restores relationship with his followers as exemplified in Thomas and Peter.

Session Preparation ■

Have on hand a study Bible, a Bible commentary, a Bible dictionary, a concordance, and hymnals for the group.

Choose from among these activities and discussion starters to plan your lesson.

An Ultimatum ■

Review by rereading John 20:19-23. Imagine that you are one of the disciples present. How do feel about this appearance?

John 20:24–21:25

In our two passages for consideration today, Jesus comes to help clear away uncertainties held by Thomas and Peter. Thomas remains uncertain that Jesus has risen from the dead. Peter is uncertain about his damaged relationship with the Lord. They are both "foggy" about a few things that prevent them from "taking off" with the Lord on the crucial journey of Christianity. As he did with Mary at the tomb, the two disciples in Emmaus, and the disciples in Jerusalem, Jesus came personally to "clear up" a few things with Thomas and Peter. Let's begin with Thomas.

An Ultimatum

A week before, Jesus had appeared to the other disciples as they huddled in fear behind locked doors. To them, Jesus imparted his peace, his shalom that offers wholeness. To them, he showed his nail-scarred hands and wounded side. On them, he breathed the Holy Spirit and commissioned them to go out in his name. To them, he gave the authority to forgive sins. It was quite a day—but Thomas wasn't there to experience it.

In the span of one night, Thomas became an outsider. While he was absent, the rules had changed. The new agenda proclaimed Christ to be risen, not dead. The new agenda empowered "commissioned" disciples

Now read John 20:24-29. How are you going to break the news to Thomas that you have seen the Lord? How do you react to his vehement response? He is only asking, though perhaps more passionately, for what you have already received. How do you imagine that Jesus would have felt about that if he had heard it?

(including Thomas and the whole community of faith) with the authority to forgive sins. The new agenda spoke of the Holy Spirit as a prerequisite for discipleship. For the other disciples, this was all new and exciting news—but Thomas wasn't there to experience it.

Understandably, when these newly commissioned disciples urged Thomas to believe that Jesus had risen from the dead, Thomas said NO! The force of his answer is evident in the original Greek. He actually said, Unless I *jab* my finger into the nail holes and put my hand into his side, I will *never* believe it (John 20:25). Thomas was adamant about his need for proof. Unknowingly, Thomas issued God an ultimatum that he would soon regret.

Thomas Represents Us All

Take turns reading aloud only Jesus' words in John 20:26-27 (not the narrative). Try to read it with a different inflection so that it conveys a different attitude each time, such as gentleness, exasperation, impatience, directiveness, joyfulness, and so on. How does the experience seem to change each time Jesus speaks these words in a different tone of voice? Which tone seems the most likely to you? (We will never know for sure.)

Now do the same thing for Thomas's response in 20:28, either alone or in conjunction with the variations on Jesus' words to

Thomas Represents Us All

Was Thomas's need for proof any greater than the other disciples' need for proof a week before? The disciples only believed *after* seeing the risen Christ. Why shouldn't Thomas be given the same privilege? Why is Thomas singled out? Some scholars believe that John, the Gospel writer, simply used Thomas to represent the kind of collective doubt that all of the disciples had exhibited.

Nevertheless, the depiction of Jesus confronting the challenge of Thomas should send us into careful introspection. Thomas demanded proof. Jesus demands faith. Thomas clung to his definition of reality. Jesus' resurrection creates a new reality. Thomas demanded the same experience with Jesus that the other disciples had had. Jesus confronted Thomas's willingness to offer God ultimatums. The focus on Thomas's need is an effective means of characterizing an attitude that demands proof before surrendering to faith.

Thomas. What new insights, if any, do you gain from this exchange?

Read John 20:29. Jesus asked, "Have you believed . . . ?" The *you* is plural. He is addressing all the disciples, not just Thomas. (Furthermore, the "you" referred to is called "blessed" because you believe without having seen Jesus in person!) What makes it possible for you to believe without having seen with your own eyes? Can Thomas be faulted for wanting to see for himself? Explain.

Bible 301 ☐

Do a further character study on Thomas using a Bible dictionary and concordance. (See also John 14.) Before this encounter with Jesus, how would you describe Thomas? Now that you have tried variations within this brief exchange between Jesus and Thomas, do you have a different or more complete understanding of this disciple?

If Jesus had needed to confront Thomas about doubt on previous occasions, this encounter between them would not have seemed so surprising. In actuality, Thomas was not a chronic doubter. John begins a sketch of Thomas's personality in John 11. There, Jesus told the disciples that they needed to go back to Judea to attend to Lazarus, who was sick and dying. The disciples showed considerable alarm at the idea and reminded Jesus that a short time before, the Jews had tried to stone him there (John 11:7-8). Later, after Jesus decided to go, Thomas demonstrated his unquestioned loyalty to Christ saying, "Let us also go, that we may die with him" (John 11:16). This does not sound like a person whose faith is suspect or who typically doubts.

The next time we hear from Thomas is in John 14. In his farewell address, Jesus spoke cryptically to his disciples about leaving for his "Father's house," a place unknown to them. Thomas honestly didn't have a clue about what Jesus was talking about. "Lord, we don't know where you are going, so how can we know the way?" (John 14:5, NIV). Thomas's honest inquiry led Jesus to speak in clearer terms for them to understand. Isn't this the type of person you want on your church committees and boards—someone who will ask clarifying questions for the benefit of the entire group?

Thomas was not a "bad" person. Today, some might simply label him as "cautious." Jesus is not concerned with Thomas's past track record, however. The Lord's eyes are on the future and the vital mission that he has for Thomas and the other disciples. In order for Thomas to do this mission effectively, Jesus needed to clear away Thomas's uncertainties about Jesus' resurrection.

Releasing the Grip of Doubt ■

Why do you think Jesus bothered to provide Thomas with the proofs that he demanded? Do you think he appeared this time especially to include Thomas? (The Gospel does not seem to indicate any other purpose.) Explain. Why does Jesus confront doubt so seriously? Do you think it is more difficult for "practical" people to come to faith? to exercise faith? Discuss.

Bible 301 ☐

Look in the index to your hymnal for hymns about assurance, comfort, or trust. (Sing or say together several of them.) What message about God and Jesus' presence do you find in those hymns? Even after twenty centuries, are we any more confident than Thomas was? Explain.

Releasing the Grip of Doubt

Thomas missed the first appearance of the resurrected Jesus in the meeting house, but he was not to be disappointed a second time. The disciples gathered in that house a week later with Thomas; and once again, Jesus entered as he had before, somehow undeterred by a locked door. Again, Jesus spoke peace to them (20:26). With the other disciples convinced of his resurrection, Jesus turned his attention completely to Thomas. There are no Scripture studies here; there is no breaking of bread. Without hesitation, Jesus confronted Thomas with the proof he had been demanding: "Put your finger here; see my hands. Reach out your hand and put it into my side. Stop doubting and believe" (John 20:27, NIV).

The sight of Jesus' wounded hands and side melted Thomas's carefully considered doubts. He was outdone. Now that Jesus had produced the "proofs" that he had demanded, Thomas could only admit that this indeed was the risen Lord. "My Lord and my God!" he cried out (20:28).

This proclamation by Thomas later became a standard profession of submission to the lordship of Christ among Christians. In effect, Thomas's words represent ultimate surrender. Tacitly, he may have admitted that he should have believed the testimony of his fellow disciples and the women witnesses. Silently, he may have confessed that his ultimatum to God was out of place. Internally, Thomas may have pledged to believe and trust in Jesus as his Lord and his God from then on.

Indeed, Thomas became an important apostle in the early church. Tradition holds that he eventually established Christian communities in Parthia, Persia, and India. To this day, some Christian churches in India claim that their origin comes from Thomas and that he was martyred in India near Madras. Jesus knows exactly what each of us needs on our faith journey. Although he would have preferred that Thomas believe out of faith without needing to see him, Jesus, nevertheless, provided what Thomas needed. As noted in the last chapter, the full belief and support of the Eleven was vitally important. Now that he had secured the faith of the Eleven, Jesus needed to make an additional appearance for Peter's sake.

The Subtle Message

Form two teams and read John 20:30-31. Team One will identify and list the "level 1" information in the John 20:19-29 passage that has already been examined. Team Two will dig into "level 2" to see the more complete meaning of how these signs are written for you to believe. What deeper insight has John provided into God's purpose and desires for all disciples, then and now?

The Subtle Message of John's Gospel

Scholars agree that the Gospel of John reveals a mature style laced with irony, subtlety, and word plays. Consequently, John must be read on two levels.

At the surface level, his message comes across in narrative mode. At a deeper level, he wrote to establish or reinforce some theological claim. This means that the words and concepts in John often have multiple interpretations. With this in mind, we must read with a keen eye for the depth and symbolic meanings he placed throughout his account.

We need to bear in mind one added bit of information before we begin. Scholars generally agree that the Gospel of John originally ended at John 20:30-31. Chapter 20 ends in triumph with the commissioning of the disciples. Then comes Chapter 21, an epilogue, likely written by John or by a member of the same Christian community.

Gone Fishin'

Read John 21:1-3. What reasons might Peter have had for returning to his former occupation of fishing?

Tell stories about ways that you have coped with difficult situations. Is there a special place, activity, person, music, or food to which you reach for comfort or aid? What is it about that "comforter" that you find helpful or soothing?

Does it occur to you to seek out the "Comforter" (John 14:26, King James Version) first? (*Comforter* is also translated as "Holy Spirit," "Advocate," "Helper," and "Counselor" in other Bible translations.) Would you have expected Peter and the others to have sought first the presence of the Holy Spirit rather than to take refuge in the familiar? Explain.

Bible 301

Look up John 21:4-14 in a Bible commentary or in your study Bible notes and research the importance and meaning of the 153 fish. Imagine that you are on the boat. How heavy is the net? How much space would the fish take up on your boat? How hard was it to pull the net in? What are you going to do with many more fish than you can possibly eat? Would Jesus provide such a large catch if he thought part of it might be wasted?

Gone Fishin'

John reports in Chapter 21 the fourth post-Resurrection appearance to the disciples. By now they believed he had been resurrected from the dead, and they had been entrusted to "forgive and retain sins." Still, they found themselves falling back into their old occupations and old ways of living. We find Peter in this passage taking comfort, perhaps, in the familiar and the practical—he went fishing with several of the other disciples (John 21:2-3). We might assume that they still needed to earn a living, but their eagerness to accompany Peter shows that perhaps they had not yet made the mission of Christ their first priority.

Fishing was familiar for Peter. It probably made him feel useful and fulfilled. Because it was his occupation, he still may have identified himself *first* as a fisherman. Jesus needed him to become a fisher of people.

Though this ambitious group of anglers toiled all night, they caught nothing. As the sun was rising, Jesus called out to them to cast the net on the right side of the boat instead. They failed to recognize that it was the Lord, but they obeyed him anyway.

Jesus' command to cast the net in again has a dual meaning. On the surface, it highlights our need to obey Christ, though it may seem pointless. On another level, John strikes at the need to be willing to risk our reputations for Christ. Peter and crew had been fishing all night, obviously the preferred time to fish. Now, it was past daybreak when experienced fishermen would have been heading for shore.

Someone (Jesus) told them to throw their nets out one more time, this time on the right side of the boat. They could have told this "stranger" to mind his own business.

They could have responded in pride saying, "Look mister, we're professionals; we've worked these waters for years, and the fish just aren't here today." Instead, they suspended judgment and obeyed Christ's "absurd" command. Amazingly, they made a great catch of 153 fish.

The Symbolism of Fishing

The Symbolism of Fishing ■

What symbolic and subtle meanings might John have been conveying with his use of fish and fishing?

Bible 301 □

Look up fish, fishing, and fishermen in a Bible dictionary to better understand the skills required for and the place of fishing in the indigenous industry. (You may need to look up trade, for example.) How does what you know about the occupation help you understand the metaphor of "fishing"?

What would it take for you to feel as if you are a "fisher for people"? Do you feel comfortable with that "occupation"? Explain.

John's spotlight on fish is by design. By the time that he wrote this chapter, it is likely that the Christian community was commonly using the fish as a symbolic Christian sign. The Christians used it as an acrostic. The Greek word meaning "fish" is *ichthus*. These letters form the words, *Iesous CHristos THeou Uios Soter*, which means "Jesus Christ, Son of God, Savior." The early church commonly called Christ "the fish."

John uses fish and fishing as a vehicle to convey multiple meanings. Without understanding these meanings, we cannot fully grasp the theological thrust of Jesus' probing conversation with Peter in John 21:1-14. According to *The New Interpreter's Bible (Vol. IX*, Abingdon Press, 1995):

"The symbolic relationship between the miraculous catch of fish and the disciples' mission does not seem to lie in the description of the quantity of fish, however, but in Peter's action in hauling in the net. The verb "to haul" (*helkō*) ... is the same verb used in 6:44 to describe those who come to Jesus from God ('No one can come to me unless *drawn* by the Father who sent me') and in 12:32 to describe the salvific effect of Jesus' death ('And I, when I am lifted up from the earth, will *draw* all people to myself'). The use of this verb with reference to the disciples and the catch of fish suggests that they now join God and Jesus in drawing people to

Jesus. The catch of fish, then, marks the extension of God and Jesus' work into the disciples' work."

Jesus Restores Peter

Jesus Restores Peter

Form three small groups in order for each to read a different set of Scriptures: (1) John 13:36-38; 18:15-18, 25-27 (Peter's denials); (2) John 18:1-10 (Judas's betrayal); and (3) John 6:60-66; Matthew 26:55-56 (the disciples' desertion).

The Gospels differ on just who abandoned Jesus before and at the Crucifixion, but seem to agree by an argument of silence that most of the disciples were not present at the Crucifixion. Judas betrayed Jesus and died. Peter denied Jesus and was singled out for restoration. Most of the rest deserted, at least temporarily, and no further specific response is mentioned. How would you explain these varied consequences?

Have two volunteers re-enact the conversation between Jesus and Peter in John 21:15-17. Try to capture what you imagine to be both Jesus and Peter's attitude, posture, tone of voice, and feelings. (Do this several times with other pairs, including women, or as a "fishbowl" exercise with one pair and others as observers.)

There were a few things that had been left unsaid, and now was the time to clarify them. One major concern was Peter's relationship with the Lord. Shamefully, he had denied Christ three times—something that Jesus had predicted. Of course, all the disciples had pledged their allegiance to Jesus, and all had forsaken him in some way. Nevertheless, Peter, who was emerging as perhaps the most prominent leader among the disciples, had dramatically denied his Lord.

Disappointment and shaken trust in relationships can be overcome—if it is honestly addressed. In all of the excitement of seeing the resurrected Jesus, Peter and the Lord evidently had never talked about Peter's denial. Left unattended, Peter's lingering memories could have destroyed his self-confidence. Would he run away the next time that his loyalty to Christ was tested? Would he ever believe that Christ could fully trust him? John may have included Chapter 21 in part to show us the power of divine restoration.

The restoration began with the meal on the beach. The meal with this "stranger" was similar to the account in Luke of the Emmaus road travelers. John reports the same lack of recognition among the disciples (John 21:9-13). Apparently all was revealed during the meal, though John doesn't tell us. He simply moves along his narrative, clearly implying that Peter understood who this stranger is.

After a meal of bread and fish, Jesus questioned Peter about their relationship (21:15-

For "Peter": Why do you think Jesus kept asking you if you loved him? Why did you respond with the word meaning "like" rather than with "love"? Do you have any lingering thoughts about your denial of Christ after he was arrested?

For "Jesus": What were you trying to convey to Peter? Do you think he understood? Why did you ask three times? What did you mean in asking Peter to feed your sheep?

For "observers": What feelings, attitudes, body language, and insights did you observe? Do you think any of your own answers would be different from Jesus or Peter's? Explain. Confrontation is always costly. What could be lost and what could be gained in this confrontation between Jesus and Peter?

Follow Me!

Read John 21:18-23. How would you respond if Jesus told you that your following him would mean dying a martyr's death? What does "Follow me" mean to you? Is there a point beyond which you will not follow? Explain.

Peter was chided for asking about John's future. Is it appropriate to ask in prayer about the discipleship (or faith journey) of someone else? to compare your own

17). It is a most interesting conversation in the Greek. Jesus asked Peter, "Do you love me?" using the word *agapan*, a term that means "unconditional love." Peter responded using a lesser word, *philein*. In effect, Peter said, "Yes Lord, you know that I *like* you." This happened again. The third time, Jesus used Peter's word, *philein*. "Simon, son of John, do you *like* me?

That final change of wording unnerved Peter. If I were Peter, I would be squirming by now. What was Jesus asking? One can almost hear Peter's heart drop. It would be difficult to keep thoughts of his denial of Jesus from flooding his mind. If ever there was an opportune time to restore Peter's relationship, it was now.

Peter's future ministry would be full of challenges. He would suffer persecution. Paul would later confront Peter's unresolved prejudice against Gentiles. Finally, he would die a martyr's death, suggested by John 20:18-19. According to tradition, he was crucified upside down. Jesus knew that this was the time to reconcile their estranged relationship before the challenges of ministry engulfed Peter.

Follow Me!

In his next breath, Jesus said to Peter, "Follow me." In other words, follow me into the Christian calling that demands complete surrender—even to the point of death. Peter wondered if John would suffer a similar fate—misery loves company (20:20-22). In so many words, Jesus said, "If I want him to remain alive until I return, what is that to you?" That statement led some to believe that John would never die.

Peter and John had their own distinctive paths to follow, however. Jesus made it clear

Christian journey to another person's? Explain.

Close With Prayer

Pray the following prayer:

Dear Lord, we confess that we have at times acted like Thomas, making demands before we will venture into faith. Forgive us for the times that we doubt you. We must also admit that, like Peter, we sometimes feel estranged from you. In your mercy, mend any breaches in our relationship with you. By your grace, restore us to uninterrupted fellowship. Then, as you did with Peter, send us out in faith to minister with grace, mercy, and love. Amen.

that Peter must to be willing to travel along *his own* spiritual journey whether or not it proved to be more difficult and dangerous than John's. We are each called to walk with Christ according to our particular God-given gifts and graces.

Each journey has its unique challenges. There is no warrant in comparing ourselves with "the Christian next door." Jesus simply says, "Follow me—commit to the Christian pathway based on your love and trust in me." Jesus had breathed the Holy Spirit on Peter. He had given him the power to become a son of God. Jesus demands an active love from each of us. Each time Jesus asked, "Do you love me?" he commanded Peter to back it up with action. "Feed my lambs"; "take care of my sheep"; "feed my sheep" (20:15, 16, 17).

These activities involve the energy of faith, the commitment of love, and the willingness to endure hardship for the sake of Christ. "Follow me!" This imperative carries the weighty challenge of unconditional love and commitment. To we believers in the risen Christ, Jesus' words, "Follow me," challenge us to reconcile any breach in our relationship with Christ that prevents us from serving him wholeheartedly.

Session Four

Called to Conversion, Called to Serve

Session Focus ■

Two amazing phenomena occur in today's passage of Scripture: Saul's conversion and call to Christian ministry and Ananias's willingness to minister to the newly converted Saul. This session focuses on both Saul and Ananias and how the Lord's appearance affected their lives.

Session Objective ■

In this session, we will explore the dynamic ability of Christ to transform us into children of God and then press us into Christian service.

Session Preparation ■

Have on hand a Bible dictionary, such as *The New Westminster Dictionary of the Bible* (Westminster, 1970); New Testament Bible maps (may be found in a study Bible or a Bible dictionary); and hymnals for the group.

Choose from among these activities and discussion starters to plan your lesson.

Acts 9:1-19a

"Christian conversion" and "the call" to Christian service lead to internal turmoil and soul searching. In Acts 9:1-19a we find two characters confronted with the opportunity to answer the call to Christian conversion and the call to Christian service. Saul of Tarsus usually gets all of the attention in this passage, but Ananias also deserves a mention.

In this chapter, the biblical scene is drastically different from those in the previous three chapters. Up to this point, we have been exploring encounters between the risen Christ and his disciples in the few weeks following the Resurrection when the risen Jesus appeared to his disciples. Now we move forward about two years. Acts 9 reports that Saul saw a flash of light from heaven and heard the voice of the Lord. Still, Saul, later known as Paul (Acts 13:9), insisted that he *saw* the Lord (1 Corinthians 9:1). The other distinction is that Saul was not a disciple of Christ.

A Destructive Force

The opening verse of Acts 9 spills us into a tension-filled time of persecution for Christians. "Meanwhile, Saul was still breathing out murderous threats against the Lord's disciples . . . [and] went to the high priest" (Acts 9:1, NIV). By this time, Saul

A Destructive Force

Divide these Scriptures among three small groups: (1) Acts 2:22-23; (2) Acts 1:15; 2:4, 47; 4:4; 5:14; 6:7; (3) Acts 7. What might these passages suggest about why Saul was so violently angry with the Christians? What threat did the church present to Saul and the leaders of Judaism?

Consider this case as a means to thinking about the turmoil within Jewish circles. Jesse Cristo grew up in your church and everyone knew him. After college, he began to take a serious interest in his faith, and church members thought that was wonderful. He started sharing his beliefs in earnest with his friends, and then his friends' friends. Then he began pushing his friends to a commitment to radical justice and fairness for everyone, including those outside your church. At the same time, he began to criticize church members for being lax in their own level of commitment. Then his friends claimed he performed some miracles, and Jesse claimed that he would be killed for what he was doing—and he was right. Jesse's friends blamed church members for some level of complicity in his death. They took up the mantle and spread out over the state and beyond doing what Jesse had urged and modeled. Some of them were reported to have done miracles as well.

was driven obsessively by his passion to annihilate the church. Why had his anger reached such a feverish pitch? Perhaps Christianity threatened his religion and his position in life as a Pharisee. Peter and other Christians were boldly denouncing the Jews and accusing them of killing the true Messiah (Acts 2:22-23). One of the characteristics of Christ's church is its ability to reveal selfishness and corruption in human systems. These reasons would have been more than sufficient to ignite Saul's anger.

From the initial surge of converts on the Day of Pentecost, the church had been growing rapidly (Acts 1:15; 2:4, 47; 4:4; 5:14; 6:7). At the outset, many Jewish leaders considered the new believers as an annoying, fanatical sect of Judaism. As their numbers grew, however, the new doctrines and faith practices of the church emerged. The radically different Christian teachings made it clear that these proponents of Christianity were more than mere misguided Jews. They were a growing movement that was quickly establishing itself as an influential new religion.

Left unchallenged, this spreading belief in the resurrected Christ could turn the masses against the Hebrew religion for its failure to recognize the Messiah, its rejection of Jesus' ministry, and its complicity in his crucifixion. The leading groups and institutions within Judaism would suffer humiliation, possibly a reduction in power and influence. The Sanhedrin, the council that tried and sentenced Jesus to death as a false prophet, could become suspect itself (Luke 22:66-71). While Saul was not a member of the Sanhedrin, he did enlist their help while he was persecuting the Christians (Acts 9:1-2, 14; 22:4-5).

What do you think of Jesse's "movement"? Do you want to join? How do you feel as a church member about having been criticized, at least obliquely? about taking the blame for his death? about being pushed to an intensive commitment in your own discipleship? Did Jesse really perform miracles? How did other church members regard him?

The Force of Courage

Choose one (or more) of Peter's sermons to begin to examine the courage of the early disciples. See Acts 2:14-40; 3:12-26; or 4:8-12. What was Peter's central message? Thinking about the context in which it was delivered, how might it have been threatening? Does the church appear to be a threat to anyone today? Have others ever felt threatened because of your expression of faith in Christ? Explain.

When Saul had heard that some Christians had escaped to Damascus, he asked for letters of introduction to the synagogues in Damascus. According to 1 Maccabees 15:15-21 (the Apocrypha), the Romans had apparently granted to the high priest, as leader of the Sanhedrin, power to extradite Jewish fugitives who had fled Jerusalem for Damascus, which had a sizable Jewish population. It is perhaps this policy to which Luke refers.

The Force of Courage

The determination of Christ's followers was another source of irritation for Saul. From the first several chapters of Acts, it would appear that the followers of the Way, as they were then known (Acts 9:2), were often in conflict with the Jewish officials. Apparently, however, the jails could neither hold them nor deter them from proclaiming Christ. The more they were questioned, beaten, or jailed, the more their numbers grew and the more close-knit the group became.

Courageously, the early Christians often used their clashes with the Jewish leaders as an opportunity to preach to the crowds that usually gathered. Peter preached to the crowds that gathered to see the spectacle on the Day of Pentecost (Acts 2:14-40). He preached again after the beggar was healed at the Temple (Acts 3:12-26), and again when they were arrested (Acts 4:8-12). The messages were all similar: God sent Jesus as the fulfillment of all the Hebrew Scripture prophecies, but the Jewish leaders rejected him and crucified him. He was not defeated. God raised Jesus from death, and he is both Lord and Christ.

Persecution Escalates

Without looking up the story in Acts 7, see how much of it you remember. Use a ball or another small object to keep the story going. One person will start, give a sentence or two of the story, and throw the "ball" to another person who will continue. Anyone who wishes can "pass" by tossing the ball to someone else.

Then look up the story of the stoning of Stephen in Acts 7. How much of it did you remember? What was the essence of Stephen's sermon that angered so many people? What events placed Stephen in the position of danger? What did Stephen do that caused more persecution to break out against the Christians? How did the first-century Christians respond to conflict and persecution?

Bible 301 ☐

In a Bible dictionary, look up Dispersion (or diaspora) to learn more about how Jews scattered across the known world. Using a map, as in The Westminster Dictionary of the Bible (Westminster Press), locate the largest settlements outside Jerusalem. According to this dictionary, there were about 2.5 million Jews in Jerusalem and almost half again that

Persecution Escalates Because of Stephen

Peter was not the only one whose Christian message indicted the Jewish leadership. It was the message of the newly emerging church, and it angered many of the Jews. These and similar encounters continued throughout the history of the first-century church. Though hostile, the two groups were able to coexist in Jerusalem until an unforgettable encounter with a new deacon named Stephen took place.

When Stephen was arrested and false witnesses testified against him, he did as so many others had done. He preached about Jesus (Acts 7:1-53). His sermon was so persuasive and so harsh in its indictment of the Jews that he was stoned to death (7:54-60). This marked the beginning of a persecution that caused members of the church to flee, but it also resulted in the spread of the gospel outside of Jewish boundaries (8:1b).

A young Jewish man named Saul was present for Stephen's stoning. He looked after the coats of the witnesses while they stoned Stephen to death. As a devout Jew, belonging to the strict sect of the Pharisees, Saul was unable to contain his righteous indignation after Stephen's sermon. As far as he was concerned, it was blasphemy to say that a troublesome carpenter's son of questionable heritage, who died an ignoble death, was the Son of God and the Messiah. He responded by going out of his way to imprison both men and women who embraced these new beliefs (Acts 8:3; 9:1-2; 22:4-5; 26:9-11). By the religious standards of the time, Saul was a moral man who thought he was doing a good thing.

number elsewhere by the first century. The belief in resurrection would have spread with them. As Christians fled Jerusalem, news of the resurrection of Jesus would go with them as well.

Look up Acts 8:3; 9:1-2; 22:4-5; 26:9-12—reports of Saul's persecution. Where did he go? What did he do? Acts 9:2 includes the fact that Saul wanted to arrest both men *and* women. Why do you think Luke chose to include that detail? How did Saul justify his actions?

Had he been pursuing you, what do you think you would have done?

Confrontation on the Road ■

Imagine that you are one of Saul's traveling companions. (You can choose the Acts 9 or the Acts 22 version). You have brought Saul to a Damascus inn and some of the locals are asking about what happened. What did Saul tell you about his own experience? How does it square with what you experienced? Saul is blind, fasting, and resting in his room. What do you think is going through his mind right now?

Confrontation on the Damascus Road

By the time we meet Saul again, on the Damascus road, belief in the bodily resurrection of Christ had spread throughout many of the regions where Jews lived outside of Israel. In Acts 9, we see the picture of a man who was consumed by the fires of his own righteousness "breathing out murderous threats against the Lord's disciples" (Acts 9:1, NIV). Untold numbers of both men and women were placed in prison because of Saul's misguided convictions.

Little did Saul know how quickly his anger would be turned to awe. Now as he approached Damascus, something totally unexpected happened. Saul encountered the risen Christ. A light from heaven blinded him, and he fell to the ground, stunned. Lying in the dust in the road, Saul heard a voice say to him, "Saul, Saul, why do you persecute me?" (Acts 9:4).

It is important to note that Saul's encounter with the risen Christ took place about two years after the Resurrection and long after his Ascension. If Jesus Christ was no longer walking among people at that time, some may ask, How he could have appeared to Paul? Some Bible scholars believe that Paul was struck by lightning and/or had something akin to an epileptic seizure, which caused him to hallucinate.

We are not helped by Saul's traveling companions. By Saul's account in Acts 9:7, they heard the voice but saw nothing; his retelling in Acts 22:9 says that they saw the light but heard nothing. However, by both accounts, the companions apparently knew something had happened, even if they did not understand what it was. Saul insisted that he did see Jesus, either literally (1 Corinthians 9:1) or figuratively in his epiphany moment with the voice and light from heaven (Acts 9:1-9; 22:6-9).

Saul's encounter with Christ on the Damascus road is significant for a number of reasons. Most important, it validated him for apostolic ministry. The Twelve were declared apostles because they had been called by Jesus, had been with Jesus throughout his ministry, and had witnessed his resurrection. Though Saul had not been with Jesus throughout his ministry, he now had experienced a call. Due to Jesus' appearance, Saul could say with confidence that he too had seen the Lord. Like the other disciples, the risen Lord empowered Saul with the Holy Spirit and commissioned him.

A Changed Man ■

Now try to look at this event through Saul's eyes. You have been persecuting Christians; Jesus has accused you of persecuting him. You thought you were doing the right thing. Now how do you feel and why? What is it that has changed your convictions so dramatically? Why is Jesus' appearance to so significant?

Continue to place yourself in the position of Saul. You are praying and fasting in your room, still blind. With a partner, take some quiet time to talk about your Damascus road experience. (This can also be done as a journaling exercise if you can write and still imagine that you are blind!)

What spiritual purpose, if any, can be served by your physical blindness? Since a prevailing belief is that

A Changed Man

Christ's appearance to Saul made an indelible impact on him. In his later writings, he clearly understood that he was an apostle based on his divine call from Christ. He was an apostle, "sent neither by human commission nor from human authorities, but through Jesus Christ and God the Father, who raised him from the dead" (Galatians 1:1).

Jesus Christ's appearance to Saul on the Damascus road can best be explained as a mystery. The indisputable fact is that Christ is able to employ ways of revealing himself to us that we have not even imagined. Somehow, on the road to Damascus, Jesus made himself known to Saul; and it changed his life and Christian history—forever!

Saul's encounter with the risen Christ revealed his personal shortcomings. He had been zealous for the wrong cause. He was destroying the very work that God was trying to promote. Like Moses, Saul now recognized how flawed humanity is. When blindness or other physical infirmities are the result of sin, what else might your blindness mean to you? How about the voice you heard?

Your companions had a different experience; you got something they didn't get, and they are really confused. What are you going to say to them about all this? How do you think they are going to take it?

Saul fasted for three days following his encounter with Christ. In what ways might Saul have benefited from this time of fasting? Is fasting a spiritual discipline that you observe?

Read Acts 22:3-5; 26:9-11. Paul discovered he was going the wrong way and determined to change. Have you ever had a strong interior conviction that you were right about an important principle, value, behavior, or course of action and then discovered that not only was it not right but others were being hurt by it? If you feel comfortable, tell about that situation and what you did about it. What role did faith in God play in the situation and how you evaluated that situation? How did you go about making a decision to do or be something different? Were there any "traveling companions" who could offer help or support?

Moses encountered the "I AM" speaking from a burning bush, his flawed past as a murderer humiliated him. "Lord, who am I that I should go?" (Exodus 3:11). He had lost credibility in the Pharaoh's household; who was he to serve God? Similarly, Saul must have gazed remorsefully at his personal deficiencies.

In the presence of the Lord, Saul quickly learned that he had wronged many people and had inadvertently persecuted the Lord for what he had thought were noble reasons. In utter dismay, Saul cried, "Who are you Lord?" Jesus Christ replied, "I am Jesus, whom you are persecuting" (Acts 9:5). It was there that Saul discovered how "blind" he had been to the truth of the Resurrection.

There is a subtle message of hope and solidarity housed in Jesus' response to Saul's question. Saul had been persecuting Christians who had risked their reputations and lives to proclaim Christ as risen Lord. Ironically, however, Jesus' response to Saul would lead one to think that Saul had been persecuting Jesus personally, not his followers; and he soon found out that the risen Christ was more than equal to the challenge.

Saul's Damascus road encounter illustrates another crucial principle for us to consider. Without leadership from God, even our best intentions can yield disastrous results. Every time Saul (Paul) told his conversion story, he confessed that he was working hard at doing the wrong things until he met Jesus, even though he felt at the time that they were right (Acts 22:3-5; 26:9-11). Simply said, Scripture teaches us that without Christ, all human beings are busily traveling on a one-way street—in the wrong direction. As we look at the spiritual blindness that made it possible for Saul to persecute Christians, it should cause us to look long and hard at some of the things we do.

Saul's Conversion ■

Examine the ways we can talk about conversion: in a single moment or over a span of time.
How can you determine whether someone has truly been converted to Christ? Who should make the judgment about the validity of conversion? Is conversion something that happens only once or something that can occur many times? Explain.

Take a few minutes to share briefly your own story of coming to a conviction in Jesus Christ. Were there stages or "movements" in your encounter with the Spirit? Was your life changed in any way, even briefly, because of these encounters?

Saul's Conversion

Saul's encounter with the risen Christ permanently changed his life. From that moment forward, Saul's life acquired a different agenda. His old venomous accusations about Christianity dried up. His previous understanding about Jesus began to be redefined. His prized position as a Pharisee no longer provided the complete assurance in his religious and spiritual outlook that it once had. Jesus brought him to a place of new beginnings. Together, Saul and the Lord would rebuild Saul's life on the solid ground of faith in Christ.

When did Saul's conversion take place? Scholars are often divided over this subject. Some suggest that Saul's encounter with Christ and his realization of sin qualified as a converting moment. Others argue that Saul was confronted with his sins immediately but not repentant until his conversation with Ananias three days later. The question of *when* someone is converted to Christianity remains a thorny issue for many today.

Some people testify to a specific time and date of their conversion, that moment in which they realized with conviction that Jesus is Lord and Savior. Others have been raised in the faith and have "grown into" that belief and assurance. Yet others may spend days, months, even years, wrestling internally with their faith until a "reachable moment," when they see how life paths and faith fragments finally coalesce with clarity and conviction. Conversion is a process.

Conversion, like an encounter with Christ, is also a mystery. After hearing Jesus speak to him, Saul lost his sight. Nevertheless, in his brief time of physical blindness, he could understand ("see") with more clarity than ever before. The Lord literally placed him in a situation that enabled Saul to "see" just what Jesus Christ wanted him to see.

The Holy Spirit at Work

As one well versed in the Jewish Scriptures, Saul had much to reflect on. Like the first witnesses who saw the risen Christ, Saul was given the opportunity to remember what the Scriptures said about the Messiah. Saul needed to make his own personal application.

It is also likely that Saul understood his blindness as punishment for tirelessly persecuting Christians and the cause of Christ. Jewish belief commonly understood personal sin as a cause of physical sicknesses. However, throughout this trying time for Saul, the process of repentance was at work. Repentance is a two-part process. It involves first a genuine remorse over one's sins, and second a turning to Jesus Christ in faith and belief. For three days, the Lord provided Saul with the solitude he needed to ponder the implications of his actions against Christ and the church. In the process, his pharisaic pride was being eroded as his new faith in Christ found root in his soul.

During that same three-day period, he neither ate nor drank. Fasting is another way of improving our "spiritual hearing." Without the "distraction" of eating, our attention can focus on prayer and fellowship with the Lord. We know that Saul spent this time praying because of the Lord's conversation with Ananias in a vision. The Lord said to Ananias, "Get up and go to the street called Straight, and at the house of Judas look for a man of Tarsus named Saul. At this moment he is praying" (Acts 9:11).

The Holy Spirit at Work

Review the Scriptures about Stephen and Saul (Acts 7 and 9). How do you see the Holy Spirit at work? How has the Spirit intervened directly or brought together particular people and circumstances to advance God's will?

Bible 301

Look in the index to your hymnal and identify hymns that refer to the Holy Spirit. Sing a few of your favorites, if you wish.

What do these lyrics covey about the work of the Holy Spirit? What sense of mystery do they impart or in what ways do they impart the truth behind the mystery so that God's presence is revealed?

Think about your own encounters with the Holy Spirit or moments that you would describe as points of conversion, conviction, or assurance. Spend some quiet time journaling about your experience with God in those events or times. Were you praying at the time? working on a social justice issue? digging in the garden? In how many different venues do you sense God's powerful and personal presence?

Christ knows how to bring pride to its knees. With a flash of light, the Lord demonstrated his unquestionable divinity by taking away Saul's sight and later restoring it through the hands of a man whom Saul would have persecuted a few days before. Like the disciples on that first Easter Sunday, Saul may have needed some demonstration to provide irrefutable "proof" that he was dealing with the risen Savior. When Ananias met Saul, Saul was praying to the Lord whom he once despised. Humility and repentance had born fruit in this once zealous Pharisee.

Ananias to the Rescue

Encounter with the risen Christ is not restricted to those in need of salvation. Ananias, who was already a Christian, found himself in the middle of a challenging encounter with the Lord. Jesus called upon Ananias to minister to Saul. Ananias's first reaction was a flat refusal: "Lord, I have heard from many about this man, how much evil he has done to your saints in Jerusalem; and here he has authority from the chief priests to bind all who invoke your name" (Acts 9:13-14). The Lord used this encounter with Ananias as an opportunity to develop greater trust from Ananias. As a believer, Ananias was to trust Christ and obey his commands.

This encounter was a fitting test of discipleship for Ananias. If he chose to obey Christ, he risked suffering physical harm or imprisonment. If he chose to protect his personal safety, he would reap God's displeasure. At this point, Ananias did not know if Saul was still seething with anger, or if he had actually been converted to Christ. In the face of his fears, he had the assurance that things would be radically different!

Ananias to the Rescue ■

Read Acts 9:10-19a. With four other people, re-enact this part of the story. You might have Ananias and the Lord on one side of the room and Saul and the Holy Spirit on the other, each having their own vision. Use your own words to convey the biblical text. Observers can watch while both visions play out. What nuances or interpretations come to you through this re-enactment?

Bible 301 ☐

Look up Ananias *in a Bible dictionary. Why is he an important figure? What else do you now know about him that helps you understand his relationship in Acts 9 with Saul and the early church leaders?*

What initial reservations did Ananias have about going to minister to Saul? Have you ever doubted that someone with a questionable past had actually been converted to Christianity? How did you overcome your doubts?

Ananias was afraid of Saul, and for good reason. Assume that you are Ananias or the brother or sister of Stephen and know Saul has had a hand in the persecution or death of a loved one. Write a letter to Saul expressing your reaction to his recent conversion to Christianity.

By agreeing to minister to Saul, did Ananias face any genuine danger? How costly has it been for you to serve Christ? What vital message did Jesus instruct Ananias to take to Saul? How did he approach Saul? What might it have cost Ananias personally to address him as "Brother Saul"? What specific action by God indicated that Saul had become a child of God? Explain.

What is the significance of Saul's baptism? What is the spiritual significance of baptism to you?

The Call to Christian Service

Compare your church's openness and your own against this series of questions: "Where can former violent offenders go?" Is Saul's dramatic turnaround a model or inspiration to

Ananias's plea failed to dissuade the Lord from his goal. Christ had a commission for Saul; Ananias was to carry the message. Jesus wanted Saul to serve him by making the Lord's name known to Gentiles and kings and to the people of Israel. Ananias knew even before Saul did that this would be no picnic (Acts 9:15-16).

Thankfully, Ananias won his personal battle against doubt and obeyed the command from his vision. The evidence of his internal victory was apparent when he first met Saul. Immediately, Ananias placed his hands on him, called him "Brother Saul," and validated Saul's vision of the risen Christ. Ananias accepted Saul because Christ had accepted him. Ananias's openness in the face of fear (and reason) is a shining example to us in trust and godly obedience despite the personal cost.

Later, Saul would repeatedly link his call to service with his conversion experience. In Acts 22:6-16, Saul recalled his Damascus road conversion. The sequence is telling. First, he asked, "Who are you, Lord?" (Acts 22:8). After discovering that Jesus had spoken, his next question was, "What am I to do, Lord?" (Acts 22:10). The early church grew so quickly because Christians understood the necessity of serving Christ. Once they clearly understood *who* Jesus was, they desired to know *what* to do for the Lord. Christianity continues to need people who will answer the call to conversion and the call to serve.

The Call to Christian Service

Christian discipleship is costly. We may have to sacrifice our safety, our reputations, our finances, or even our lives. Like Ananias, we never know if the person God asks us to visit will be receptive or hostile, even dangerous. Perhaps for the first time, Ananias

you to push your own boundaries of acceptance and sense of mission? Explain.

Would you say that you have answered the call to Christian conversion and the call to Christian service? If not, you may wish to offer personal prayers to the Lord now.

Close With Prayer

Ask for specific prayer requests related to Christian conversion and Christian service. Close by praying:

Dear Lord, we stand knowing that you call us to conversion and Christian service. We come before you in need of a divine encounter and so we use the words of the psalmist: [Read aloud Psalm 51: 10-15].

had to trust Christ's ability to transform the life of "his enemy."

The contemporary Christian church faces the same challenge of trusting the conversion process. Where can former violent offenders go to church and feel welcome long enough for conversion to take place? How far do we trust the former thief who claims that he "got saved" while doing time? When someone with a questionable past says she has been converted, what perceptions or prejudices must we overcome to believe her? Likewise, Saul is our exemplary example of the thoroughness of Christian conversion. He received his sight from the hands of a man he once would have condemned to prison. As a sign of adoption and commissioning for service, Jesus empowered Saul with the Holy Spirit. Then, as a sign of complete renunciation of his former ways, Saul was baptized into the faith he had so bitterly opposed. The mystery of Christ's ability to transform our lives and place us into his service remains powerful today. It is all possible because, as the apostle Paul says, "If the Spirit of him who raised Jesus from the dead is living in you, he who raised Christ from the dead will also give life to your mortal bodies through his Spirit, who lives in you" (Romans 8:11, NIV).

Session Five

Ringside Seats at "The Great Debate"

Session Focus ■

This session explores the "great debate" between the Sadducees and Jesus regarding the resurrection of the dead. Jesus tells the Sadducees and us the way to prepare for the resurrection—become a faithful child of God.

Session Objective ■

In this session, group members will discover some of the fundamental beliefs associated with resurrection. Group members should be inspired to explore the priorities that govern the way they live presently and to consider their readiness to face the Lord in eternity.

Session Preparation ■

Have on hand a Bible dictionary and at least one Bible with an Apocrypha to use for the *Bible 301* activities.

Choose from among these activities and discussion starters to plan your lesson.

Luke 20:27-40

In today's session, the focus of our study shifts from Christ's resurrection appearances to the resurrection of the dead in its broader sense. What happens to us after we die? Will we have the same bodies? Will we still relate as husband and wife? Will we have to account for what we did throughout our lives? The questions are endless and useful. Our natural curiosity about eternity should encourage us to learn more about resurrection and what it entails. We will start the process of discovery with the great debate between Jesus and the Sadducees.

Who Were the Sadducees?

The Sadducees were a small but powerful group, haughty and therefore despised by the masses. Nonetheless, they held high posts as priestly aristocrats, yet they thought nothing of living in close contact with the oppressive Roman rulers. By associating with the Romans, the Sadducees thought they could promote the *secular* interests of the people. They were liberal in terms of their secular agenda, but very conservative religiously. No Jewish religious group had a greater investment in preserving the status quo than the Sadducees. They were strict legalists: only the law of Moses was valid in their regard.

The Sadducees' brutal enforcement of the

letter of the law made people shudder. The Pharisees, generally laypersons and community leaders, explained the Mosaic demand, "an eye for an eye and a tooth for a tooth," metaphorically. They allowed people to satisfy an offense by paying a monetary penalty. By contrast, the Sadducees literally demanded an eye or a tooth! The Sadducees required a widow actually to spit into the face of the brother-in-law who refused to marry her under the prescribed levirate marriage rights (Deuteronomy 25:7-9). If someone bore false witness against another person, the Sadducees demanded death.

The Sadducees commonly wore gold and other finery, while the Pharisees and Essenes disciplined themselves to wear modest attire. To maintain their well-to-do status, the Sadducees clearly had a personal stake in maintaining their present status quo.

The Sadducees were literalists, that is they believed and enforced the Mosaic law. Do you feel secure within the boundaries of a specific set of beliefs? Do you feel constrained within those boundaries? Explain.

Refer to Deuteronomy 25:7-9. What do you think of the specific requirements to follow the law literally? What impact might there be in the faith community if infractions of the biblically mandated and culturally prescribed behavior were noted with what we would regard today as uncivil behavior?

Patrons and Power ■

The patron/client system placed the Sadducees in a dual position as both client of Rome and patron of the general population. In what ways are you in a patron/client system? Are there any arenas in your life in which you answer to one power structure but have a leadership role in another system? If so, how do you deal with the differences in power? in personal relationships? How do you exercise your power?

Patrons and Power

The Sadducees' political alliances with the Romans afforded them further position and power. They had achieved a kind of "top dog" status in Hebrew society. The idea of status was particularly important in the patron/client world in which they lived.

The ideal of "pulling yourself up by your bootstraps" simply did not exist in the ancient Mediterranean world of the Sadducees. No one achieved success on personal merit. In that world, one needed to be connected to networks of family, friends, power brokers, and patrons.

Patrons were the elite who could provide some tangible benefit to others because of their superior power, influence, reputation, and wealth. Patrons enjoyed a considerable amount of dominance over their clients. By contrast, clients became indebted to patrons because they received some benefit from them. Patrons expected indebted clients to supply them with political support, information, and honor. The Sadducees were clients of Rome but enjoyed patron status over the Jewish peasant class.

Setting the Stage

The belief in resurrection took form in what we call the "intertestamental period," from about the second century B.C. (when the last of our Old Testament books was written) to about the mid-first century A.D. when the first of our existing New Testament letters was written. In that time of great oppression, the Jews developed the theological tenet that, if one were not vindicated in this life, there was assurance of divine justice and justification in the next.

By the time of this debate, Jewish thought regarding resurrection had splintered into several camps. Both the Pharisees and Essenes believed in two concepts: (1) resurrection and (2) punishment or rewards in eternity. The disciples, among others, believed that Israel would experience a national resurrection because of their covenant with God. In this national resurrection, Israel would be restored as a nation of prominence and world dominance in the age to come.

Clearly, Jesus did not introduce the idea of resurrection, but his teachings challenged the Sadducees' refusal to accept it. Belief in the resurrection from the dead carries serious implications: God's eternal rewards and punishments, including eternal life and ultimate accountability to God. The impact of resurrection is not just on the future, it also

Setting the Stage ■

What are the implications of a resurrection? What are the implications of a life lived without expectation of a resurrection?

Bible 301 □

Look up resurrection *and* Sadducees *in a Bible dictionary. How did this theology develop? What are its roots in Hebrew history?*

Skim thorough portions of Second Maccabees in the Apocrypha. Where do you see evidence of belief in a vindication from evil in the life to come? (See especially the gruesome 2 Maccabees 7.)

How did the Sadducees differ from the Pharisees and Essenes regarding the general resurrection?

Why do you think the doctrine of the general resurrection was a challenge to the Sadducees? If you had not had the benefit of knowing about the resurrection of Jesus, how do you think you would accept belief in a general resurrection? Would it make sense to you if it had never happened (as far as you could know)? Explain.

Form two teams. One team will read Luke 20:1-8, the other Luke 20:20-26. After briefly studying the passages compare notes on these points. Who was present? What happened? In what way was Jesus challenged? How did he respond? How might the various members of his audience (scribes, Pharisees, Sadducees, disciples, "ordinary" Temple visitors) have regarded his answer? How did these incidences set the stage for the question from the Sadducees?

The Question ■

Read Luke 20:27-40 to get a sense of the entire encounter. Then look more closely at the particular scenario and the question the Sadducees proposed (20:28-33).

Review the box that explains levirate marriage. What was it's purpose? Levirate marriage had as much, or more, to do with economy as with marriage, since it also maintained

---

affects the present. Would you continue to live oblivious to Christ's teachings if you knew you would ultimately have to explain your actions to him as Judge? With their patron status over their "indebted clients" (the peasant class), the Sadducees did not want anyone encouraging them to demand or hope for ultimate and eternal things.

Jesus' teachings about resurrection disrupted the carefully constructed world of the Sadducees. They were committed to disproving or dismissing belief in the resurrection of the dead. It is into this mass of varied beliefs that Jesus entered.

In Luke 20:21-22, the Pharisees tried to stump Jesus with their hypocritical question about paying taxes to Caesar. With skillful ease, Jesus dispensed their ploy with a simple answer, "Give to the emperor the things that are the emperor's, and to God the things that are God's" (Luke 20:25). The unexpected answer left the Pharisees in dumbfounded silence. You can almost hear the Sadducees chuckling at their misfortune. With feigned interest in Jesus' opinion, the Sadducees then took center stage, confident that they could outwit the Master.

The Question

Questions in oral cultures often come in the form of a story. With supposed interest in finding the "correct" answer to a question about the law of Moses, the Sadducees shared this hypothetical story and question. "Now there were seven brothers; the first married, and died childless; then the second and the third married her, and so in the same way all seven died childless. Finally the woman also died. In the resurrection, therefore, whose wife will the woman be? For the seven had married her" (Luke 20:29-33).

the deceased man's assets within the clan and protected the widow (who was also part of the family property). How would this arrangement be a benefit? Since the practice was observed, do you think it is a valid question?

What did the Sadducees hope to accomplish with their question to Jesus? What might a success in this question for the Sadducees mean for the scribes and the Pharissees in the group?

Many persons look forward to some kind of reunion in heaven with deceased loved ones whom they expect to recognize and with whom they anticipate some kind of relationship, akin to what it had been in life. In that light, do you think this is a valid question? Why? Though we don't practice levirate marriage, we do make provision for heirs and name children after ourselves. Is this a way of pursuing immortality? Does our society pursue immortality in any way? Discuss.

Invite stories of life after death. Many persons have at least heard accounts of persons whose heart and/or brain activity has stopped, yet who were restored to life. Many of them report having seen a bright light, recognizable loved ones who have died, a figure they assume to be God or Jesus, and a tremendous sense of peace. How do

The Sadducees posed a question for which they really did not expect an answer. Their ploy was simply to lure Jesus into a debate over "what ifs."

It may not have been an original question composed for the occasion. It is likely that the question is one that the Sadducees had used before to promote their particular belief and doctrine. Their question concerns what is known as levirate marriage, originally found in Deuteronomy 25:5-6.

Levirate Marriage

The purpose of levirate marriage was to assure the continuation of a family through child-bearing. The first-born male heir held a crucial place in the Jewish family system. The family's continued existence depended on each marriage producing a son. If the brother married and died without having any children, there was one remedy against the effect of death. His brother had to marry the widow and produce from her a male heir on behalf of the deceased brother. The first son of such a union would carry the deceased brother's name and family leadership of the deceased brother.

We might be persuaded to consider the Sadducees' problem with a degree of seriousness—if they believed in life after death. The Sadducees were not at all interested in debating the legitimacy of levirate marriage, however. Each of the Synoptic Gospel writers (Matthew, Mark, and Luke) make sure their readers understand the truth behind the question posed to Jesus. Before recounting the story, Luke says, for example, "Some

your interpretations of these "life after death" accounts color your thinking about what happens when we die? Do you think they reveal any truth about an afterlife? about the possibility of being reunited with your forebears? about the presence of God?

Jesus did not address the social elements of the question. In this case, they were not the point. What are some theological points raised by this question?

Sadducees, *those who say there is no resurrection*, came to him and asked him a question" (Luke 20:27-28a; italics added).

The Sadducees endeavored to lead Jesus on a futile journey through faulty logic. Ultimately, they hoped to prove that there is no resurrection of the dead. Presenting problems about the resurrection was a favorite form of entertainment for the Sadducees.

The Sadducees had possibly come to two logical conclusions, however. First, they reasoned that Jews only achieved immortality because their children carried on their family name. Second, they believed that Moses must not have believed in the bodily resurrection of the dead. The Sadducees reasoned that if there truly were a bodily resurrection of the dead, then there would be no need to perpetuate a family through levirate marriage.

We might think it strange that the Sadducees chose to ask a question framed in the context of resurrection—a doctrine that they did not believe. The mystery vanishes, however, when we examine the human motivation that drove this issue.

Self-Interest and Status Quo

Lead the group in an exploration of the resolve of the human will to cling to what it believes is important.

Use the brief synopsis of the movie or a personal experience as a kind of case study or use this suggestion: Your job is in an industry or business that is affected by foreign competition. A number of businesses have closed in the

Protecting Self-Interest and the Status Quo

Protecting self-interest is a natural human tendency. We all contend with our varying levels of selfishness. Whenever it seems that someone or something threatens to undermine our "rightly deserved" levels of status, power, and social standing—we commonly oppose them. Some retaliate with the vicious desperation of someone who fears for his life.

I once saw a TV movie that illustrated how fragile our status quo can be. A "yuppie" couple suffered through a series of nagging

US to move abroad. Also a growing number of immigrants in the US are available and willing to work for less than minimum wage. You are not at all certain about your own job security. Identify what you would do to protect your job if your employer adapted the company employment policies or threatened to close and move abroad.

How do your thoughts and feelings about this job security issue compare to the situation of the Sadducees who fought to maintain their social standing?

irritations, which were followed by a city-wide power outage. Real trouble started when their child needed medical help and none of the city's services were operational. The child's father could not get a written prescription and didn't have enough cash on hand to pay for it anyway. Led to believe that his home was also at risk from looters during this crisis, he felt even more desperate. When none of the usual systems worked, he finally resorted to theft and thuggery to care for and protect his family. This one significant departure from the status quo destroyed this family's world. With this in mind, one can understand how threatened the Sadducees were by Jesus and belief in resurrection.

Jesus had been preaching about the coming of a new Kingdom; that meant new adjustments. Jesus equated greatness with servanthood. He cautioned his followers not to sell their souls for earthly wealth. He promoted the spirit of the law instead of the letter of the law. Jesus' teachings that involved an interpretation (Midrash) of the Mosaic law were easily rejected by the Sadducees. More important, Jesus' beliefs posed a serious threat to the Sadducees' status, power, and social standing. Rather than consider an eternity with God, the Sadducees desperately clutched to the present.

Preoccupied With the Present

The concept of resurrection would disturb the neatly fashioned world of the Sadducees. The existence of eternal life would mean facing ultimate accountability for their actions in life. Perhaps they were abusive toward their clients. Maybe they paid more attention to acquiring wealth and power than to offering a cool drink to a thirsty traveler.

Preoccupied With the Present

Each of us enjoy or detest changes, due in large part to our personality. How do you generally handle major changes?

Assess the activities that occupy most of your time.

To help you dig into these questions, do a "round robin" inventory. Take turns in your group naming one thing that keeps you grounded (or mired) in the present. (Go around more than once, if you have time.) Include all arenas of your life: personal, professional or academic, church, spiritual, and so on. Then do a second inventory on other activities, attitudes, or values that urge you to think about the future.

When your inventories are complete, evaluate them. Are you satisfied that they are meaningful to you? to others? to God? Are there any activities that you need to change? What spiritual activities do you engage in that refocus your attention to God's priorities in life? Has your walk with Christ ever required you to make any major changes?

Share your reflections about the phrase "active inertia." Are you inert, but think that you are moving ahead? What are you doing for the Lord? How are you building the Kingdom?

Acknowledging resurrection as fact requires us to consider the future. What a difficult notion for someone preoccupied with the present!

The Sadducees just could not bring themselves to think of the kingdom of God in terms of the future. Even if there were a future resurrection, they reasoned that the resurrected life would not be any different from this life. Consequently, there would still be the need for marriage to produce male heirs to carry the family name. "So Jesus," they droned, "what is the fate of this unfortunate wife and these seven husbands who failed to produce an heir apparent?" Unfortunately for the Sadducees, they could only understand immortality in terms of maintaining the family name. For them, immortality was now. Furthermore, the Sadducees had created their preferred image of themselves and did not feel inclined to alter it for anyone—including Jesus.

Some of us give the *appearance* of moving forward in life by surrounding ourselves with flourishes of meaningless activity. Donald Sull, a professor of strategic and international management at London Business School, has coined a useful phrase, "active inertia." With this phrase, Sull exposes our tendency to remain fixed, inside comfortable activities—regardless of how ineffective they are for the future. We Christians often pride ourselves on "working for the Lord," but what are we doing? Are we building God's kingdom? Are we preparing others and ourselves for eternity?

Jesus' Provocative Response

Read Luke 20:34-35. Why do you think people feared death in biblical times? For what reasons do we fear death today?

Do you give much thought to the inevitability of your death? What impact does such thinking have on the way you live?

What does Jesus say about the way life will be in the resurrection? Will our existence change in the resurrection? Explain.

Bible 301

Look up Sheol (or Gehenna) in a Bible dictionary. If this was what the average person in Jesus' day expected after death, would you have feared dying? What about Jesus' comments would have cheered or alarmed you? Explain.

Marriage, Angels, and Worthiness

What are the two points that Jesus made about resurrection? What is the rele-

Jesus' Provocative Response

The Lord had a refreshing way of dealing with the Sadducees' meddlesome question. Jesus simply ignored it and addressed the more important issues. The question of whose husband the woman belongs to is absurd in itself. It is one thing to suggest that one, two, or even three husbands died without producing a male heir. But, to say that *all seven* husbands *and* the woman die without a child is stretching logic beyond reasonable limits.

This exaggerated example does reveal a deeper issue that consumed the people of the age—death. The only motivation for each of the other six marriages mentioned in the question was to produce a male heir. Producing a male heir alone would thwart the effects of death. Men of that age feared death particularly because it was the ultimate foe. It was the enemy that could annihilate a man's name, his family, and his heritage. Without the assurance of eternal life, a man's only security lay in perpetuating his name through his son. Jesus took this occasion to correct one of the Sadducees' faulty premises.

Life in the resurrection will not be like life presently is on earth. Jesus made a clear distinction between the present age and the one to come when he said, "Those who belong to this age marry and are given in marriage; but those who are considered worthy of a place in that age and in the resurrection from the dead neither marry nor are given in marriage" (Luke 20:34-35).

Marriage, Angels, and Worthiness

Jesus neatly sidestepped an engagement in the silly argument and began to teach, as if the question was a serious request for infor-

vance of angels to this answer? Is Jesus saying that when we die, we become angels? What does it mean to become children of God?

Bible 301 ☐

Look up angels *in a Bible dictionary. What are they? What function do they serve? Do they bear any resemblance, at least in your mind's eye, to the chubby, winged babies that often characterize angels in art?*

Is Jesus saying that some persons are worthy of the afterlife and others are not? What does it mean to "be worthy of a place in that age"? What is the role of grace in the final resurrection?

mation about resurrection and the coming age. Jesus' comment teaches two things. First, there is no need for marriage (or procreation) in the age to come. This is especially relevant in the context of the question. People will live forever. Therefore, the Jewish male would not have to "create" his own immortality by producing offspring with his wife. Immortality and eternal life are God's jurisdiction alone.

Human existence will change in the resurrection. "Indeed they cannot die anymore, because they are like angels and are children of God, being children of the resurrection" (Luke 20:36). Children of God are like angels in the resurrection. The meaning here is that just as angels are immortal and have no need for marriage and offspring, so it will be for the children of God. Equality with angels refers to eternal life, not to marriage.

The second point is the most provocative issue for the Sadducees and for us. Jesus mentions the fact that one must be *considered worthy of a place in that age*. We might imagine that the Sadducees were squirming by then. Tacitly, Jesus asked them if God would consider their lives worthy of entrance into the new age. The Sadducees faced a dilemma. If they honestly considered the question of "worthiness," they would have to assess their present lifestyle and behaviors. If they actually believed in resurrection, they would also have to believe in the coming Judgment.

Part of the reason for their question was to engage the Pharisees in a debate about resurrection. (Luke 20:1 sets the scene in the Temple, and the action seems not to move elsewhere.) Jesus' refusal to entertain their question as anything but a serious inquiry placed him and his response in an authoritative, teaching stance, and their lesson was much more compatible to the Pharisees with whom they were rapidly losing face. And things were about to get worse, at least from the perspective of the Sadducees.

Invoking the Law of Moses

Jesus' response to the Sadducees was nothing short of masterful. Knowing that they only recognized the books of Moses as authoritative, Jesus quoted from Exodus. Because Jesus used this tactic, the Sadducees could not refute the authority he used in his argument.

The quote from Exodus is the famous burning bush encounter between Moses and God. Jesus zeroed in on another telling statement in which God self-identifed as the God of Abraham, Isaac, and Jacob (Exodus 3:6). Jesus punched another hole in the Sadducees' logic. If God is *presently* the God of Abraham, Isaac, and Jacob, who are already dead, then these men must currently exist in some other place with God. Just to make sure that everyone was clear, Jesus said unequivocally that God is the God of the living. For God, all are alive. This implies that Abraham, Isaac, and Jacob are now alive.

Luke allowed the more liberal religious leaders to get in their own dig. Instead of Jesus' rebuke, "You are quite wrong" (Mark 12:27), it is a scribe who first addressed Jesus as "Rabbi" (or "Teacher") as the Sadducees did in Luke 20:27; and second, obliquely insulted the Sadducees by commenting, "You have spoken well" (20:39). After all this, the stunned Sadducees stood quietly, just as the Pharisees did earlier in the chapter.

Invoking the Law of Moses ■

Read Luke 20:37-38. This passage brings the argument in a full circle from Luke 20:1, where the Pharisees took on Jesus in their own debate and were found wanting. The Sadducees attempted to take their own turn, getting their jibe in with the Pharisees as well. It didn't work, either. What means does Jesus use to accomplish this turnaround?

Look back at Luke 20:1-8. Jesus was questioned about his authority, and he refused to discuss it. Now, at the end of this cycle, he revealed his authority as rooted in the most powerful and revered of Israel's forebears. What do you think was the effect of invoking the name of Moses and the patriarchs?

What do you consider to be the authoritative sources for your beliefs about resurrection and afterlife? What impact would the scribe's comment about Jesus speaking rightly have on the rest of the assembled listeners?

The idea of a resurrection leads us to consider soberly the idea of our worthiness in God's estimation. Today's passage reminds us that our worthiness is an element of choosing (or not) to live as children of God. In what ways are you choosing to live as a child of God on a daily basis?

Reflect on the questions in the text: "How must I live, given the reality of the coming Judgment. . . ?" and so on. What pursuits have been the most important for you as an adult? What insights from the session influence those pursuits?

Close With Prayer ▪

Take time to reflect on your relationship with Christ. Then, pray the following prayer:

Dear Lord, my life lies open and exposed to you now. You know the priorities that I hold onto dearly. Speak to my fears. Call me into a deeper, more loving relationship with you. Melt any resistance I may feel and flood my heart with your presence now; in Jesus' name. Amen.

What Does This Debate Mean for Us?

The essential principle in Jesus' response to the Sadducees is the critical need to be a child of God. The covenant that God first established with Abraham linked the two of them in special relationship. God expects no less from us. To demand concrete proof about the reality of resurrection is to miss the rich relationship that we can have with Jesus Christ for all eternity. We are left to ponder the following questions that the Sadducees contemptuously ignored. How must we live, given the reality of the coming Judgment? How does Jesus' emphasis on becoming a child of God influence the way we live presently? Do we clutch our present lives so tightly that we lose sight of eternity?

The Sadducees pursued wealth and power, because for them this life was all there was. If we believe in the resurrection and eternal life, how will we handle earthly wealth, power, and influence? The choice to live a meaningful life in loving relationship to God is ours. We have the power to decide to live a faithful life.

Session Six

Explaining the Unexplainable

Session Focus ■

This session focuses on the implications of believing in Christ's resurrection.

Session Objective ■

This session should provoke us to address the question, "What will happen to me when I die?" From this session we will also gain insight into the dual dynamic of identifying with the death of Christ to find the life in Christ.

Session Preparation ■

Have on hand a study Bible or a Bible atlas with maps, a Bible dictionary, hymnals, and a Bible commentary.

Choose from among these activities and discussion starters to plan your lesson.

Preparing for the Task ■

Make a list of concerns about death and dying and post it. Discuss the prevalence of these concerns even among people who profess faith in Jesus Christ.

1 Corinthians 15:1-26

As we discovered in our previous lesson, not everyone readily accepted the doctrine of the resurrection. Of the major leadership groups in the Hebrew tradition, the Sadducees debated about resurrection with Jesus (Luke 20:27-33) and disagreed with the Pharisees. In today's passage from First Corinthians, Paul faced a similar challenge.

Preparing for the Task

Some of the Corinthians also doubted that there was a resurrection of the dead. Throughout the Greco-Roman world, many conflicting ideas about death and the afterlife competed with the truth about the resurrection of Christ. Some in the congregation at Corinth were not firmly convinced themselves. Somehow, Paul had to persuade the Corinthian church to believe in Christ's resurrection and the general resurrection of the dead.

About twenty years had elapsed since Christ had appeared to his disciples. With his ascension to heaven, Christ formally handed his earthly ministry over to the disciples. Through their witness, the power of Christ's resurrection continued to make an impact on people's lives.

In a dramatic appearance, Jesus had shown himself especially to Paul, then in his early

Review the early life experiences of Paul. Paul was born about A.D. 10, witnessed the stoning of Stephen in Paul's very early 20's, had his conversion experience at about age 24, and spent three years in Arabia (Nabatea). He wrote the first extant book of the Bible, First Thessalonians, at about age 38 and First Corinthians at 45. If he was executed in Rome shortly after the record of his ministry indicated in Acts, he died at about age 52 around A.D. 62. How would these life experiences have prepared Paul for his life as "Pharisee of the Pharisees" and then as Christian missionary? How would his Jewish education in Jerusalem and his Hellenist upbringing in Tarsus have helped him minister to the Greco-Roman world?

Note the hallmark events in Paul's short life. What were you doing at those ages? (Granted, this is not a neat comparison because of the expanse of time, culture, and life expectancy, but allow it to provide food for thought.)

twentys, on the road to Damascus. Within three days, Christ had commissioned Paul to preach to the Gentiles (Acts 9:1-19). Two decades after receiving that commission, Paul stood as a mature apostle. Faithfully, he had been carrying out the Great Commission. Now, in the challenging environment of Corinth, a middle-aged Paul faced the dilemma of stimulating belief in Christ's resurrection. In today's passage, he employs personal testimony and persuasive argument.

Jesus used a variety of ways to reveal himself to his disciples. One of the methods he used was sharing Scripture. Jesus was dealing with Jewish disciples familiar with Old Testament Scriptures, however. Many in Paul's audience were Gentiles with no background in Jewish Scriptures. How would Paul fill that void in understanding?

We know that Paul was educated in Jerusalem, but there is no evidence that he had ever met Jesus. He would have been about twenty at the time of the Crucifixion, quite possibly having long since departed Palestine. Some scholars also suggest that Paul was a member of the Sanhedrin; but that is doubtful, since he never mentioned it in any of the accounts in which he reminded his audience of his exceptional reputation as a Pharisee. Paul did feel that his Damascus road encounter was a personal experience, a face-to-face revelation of the risen Christ; so in that sense, Paul claimed first-hand knowledge of Jesus. But neither he nor his audience had an "empty-tomb" eyewitness account. How best then to persuade his audience? He wrote them letters, laying out the systematic theological basis for resurrection.

Paul wrote to the Corinthians around A.D. 54–56, years before Mark, the earliest

What hallmark events prepared you for your life as a Christian disciple? How?

recorded Gospel account was written. That means that Paul could not refer to the Gospel accounts that we know. They did not exist. There were no written accounts of Christ's appearances to the other disciples that we know of. There were no empty-tomb narratives and no written record of Christ's ascension. Thus, of the extant biblical writings, Paul's letters are the earliest attempts to develop the doctrine of Christ's resurrection. In addition, he labored to clarify the doctrine of the resurrection of the dead. Because he had to explain these doctrines to Gentiles with widely varying religious beliefs, his task was extremely challenging.

Urgent for Paul ■

Read 1 Corinthians 15 quickly to establish the tone of Paul's comments. (You will return to this passage again to study it more closely.) How would you describe Paul's mood or attitude?

Bible 301 ☐

Paul uses the first six chapters to address concerns in the congregation before he gets around to answering the specific questions that they had apparently asked him. Read 1 Corinthians 1–6 to identify the concerns.

Return to 1 Corinthians 15:1-11. How would you describe the urgency or import of Paul's central message about resurrection?

Urgent for Paul, Beneficial for Us

In urgent tones, Paul expressed the heart of the gospel message in the opening verses of 1 Corinthians 15. "I want to remind you . . . of the gospel I preached to you. . . . By this gospel you are saved" (1 Corinthians 15:1-2, NIV). Paul's tone was that of a lawyer pressing his case: Are you believing in vain? I received this vital message personally from the Lord, a message that Scripture supports (15:3).

Paul's urgency seems to say, "Here is the message: Christ died, was buried, and was raised on the third day just as the Scriptures said he would be. As further proof of his resurrection, Christ then appeared to Peter, the disciples, and over five hundred brothers and sisters at one time, most of whom are still alive. He appeared to James, his half brother, and finally to me, Paul" (15:3b-8).

Persuading the Corinthians may have posed its difficulties for Paul, but it was certainly beneficial for us. We now have his expansive explanations of various aspects of the Resurrection.

Some may wonder about the passionate tone of Paul's argument. Two reasons are apparent. Obviously, some erroneous teaching or old beliefs lingered in the church. Doubt sprang up, polluting or confusing the minds of believers in Corinth. Paul had heard that some Christians in Corinth believed there was no resurrection of the dead. Second, Paul was vexed because he had dealt with the Corinthian church before. He had spent eighteen months there on a prior occasion. It seemed that each time he heard news of Corinth, it was always disturbing. The congregation suffered from immorality, incest, infighting, misuse of charismatic gifts, and more.

Paul was puzzled. How could a Christian dismiss the resurrection of the dead—even in Corinth's confusing religious environment? What did Paul expect them to believe? Throughout 1 Corinthians 15, Paul argues vehemently for the cause of Christ and the doctrine of the Resurrection.

What reasons may Paul have had for the passion or urgency of his message? How would you characterize Paul's relationship with the Corinthians?

Corinth ■

Review the geographic and demographic description of Corinth. What feel do you get for the city?

Consider the social environment in your local area. What are the major influences on the thinking of local people, for example, local leaders, media, radio? Are there any philosophies, beliefs, ideas, or values that seem to challenge your belief in Christianity? How do you personally respond to such challenges?

Corinth

The ancient reputation of Corinth suffered from both a noble and an ignoble past. *The New Westminster Dictionary of the Bible* describes ancient Corinth as "commercial in spirit, unwarlike, luxurious, and licentious." Corinth was a cosmopolitan and strategically located city, resting on a narrow isthmus, about four miles across. This city was an indespensible land link controlling the north-south trade routes. Another road about five feet wide was used to roll small ships and to transport goods across the isthmus from the Aegean Sea to the Gulf of Corinth, rather than making the lengthy voyage around the coast of Achaia.

Corinth was, for centuries, a bustling, commercial city, but found itself on the los-

Bible 301 ☐

Using your study Bible or a Bible atlas, locate Corinth on a map. Note its strategic location with the opportunity for a shortcut alternative for traveling around the entire coast of Achaia. What political and social advantages would this bring to the city? How would those factors affect the population, and what challenges would that pose to a Christian missionary?

Greek and Roman ■ Influence

What were some of the eclectic religious elements of the Corinthian population? How compatible were they with Paul's message of resurrection?

The Epicurean attitude of "eat, drink, and be merry, for tomorrow we die" promotes the idea of instant gratification. To what extent are you influenced to pursue immediate satisfaction in life? How does this affect your faith?
Are we living in a permissive society similar to Corinth? If so, how do you preserve your Christian integrity in such an environment?

How would you describe the relationship of body and soul in these other religions? in Christianity? If you were a Corinthian hearing about this doctrine for the first time, how could you make sense of it?

ing side in regional disputes. It was completely destroyed in 146 B.C. and virtually uninhabited until Julius Caesar rebuilt the city in 46 B.C. Veterans from the Roman army were given land in Corinth enabling them to settle there. The presence of this powerful minority injected a definite Roman influence on the city. In addition, Corinth became home to numbers of urban poor and freed slaves from all over the Greco-Roman world, who brought their religions and philosophies with them. With the Roman influence came the Roman tolerance for the existence of many foreign religious cults.

The Greek and Roman Influence

Just as Jesus used different methods to reveal himself to his disciples, Paul had to determine the best way to teach the Resurrection in Corinth. The Greek and Roman influence only complicated matters for Paul.

As the heartland of Greece, Corinth was home to Gnosticism, Cynicism, Mystery religions, Platonism, Epicureanism, Stoicism, and numerous other cults, religions, and philosophies. Two will serve to illustrate the arena into which Paul brought his Christian message.

Though the Greek philosopher Plato lived more than 400 years earlier (about 428–327 B.C.), his beliefs regarding the immortality of the soul still influenced the populace. The Greeks believed in the immortality of the soul, but refuted bodily resurrection. Some Christians in Corinth may have shared the Greek beliefs about the body. To the Greeks, the body was matter and therefore evil. Because the body was considered evil, they reasoned that there was no need for resurrection of the body.

Bible 301 ☐

*In a Bible dictionary,
research the term religion
and the specific religions
and philosophies mentioned in the text. Many
have similar tenets, especially about the dualistic
approach to body and spirit
or soul. How would these
beliefs be alike or different
from Christianity? How
might this have predisposed Paul to comment
that he approached the
Corinthians in weakness,
fear, and trembling?*

Epicureanism stood as another antagonist to the belief in bodily resurrection. Based mainly on the teachings of the Greek philosopher Epicurus, Epicureanism taught that pleasure was the supreme good and main goal of life. According to Epicurus, true happiness (not sensual enjoyment) was the serenity resulting from the conquest of fear of the gods, of death, and of the afterlife. Though the actual teaching was not based on libertinism, one result of such thought was reflected in the attitude, "eat drink and be merry, for tomorrow we die." With no belief in an afterlife, present pleasures became the preoccupation of the people.

In summary, the Corinth that Paul faced posed considerable challenges to the Christian message. The constant influx of people and ideas produced a confusing mass of beliefs about immortality and bodily resurrection. By Paul's own admission, he walked into this situation in weakness, in fear, and in much trembling (1 Corinthians 2:3).

**Erroneous
Teaching** ■

In four small groups, examine the Scriptures in this
section (1 Corinthians 4:8;
2 Timothy 2:16-18;
Ephesians 1:14; Romans
8:22). Read the specific
verse(s) and enough of the
surrounding text to understand the context.

What is the significance of
Paul's words in these passages to the notion that the
Corinthians thought they
already "got it"? that the

Erroneous Teaching About the Resurrection of the Dead

Beyond the numerous secular philosophies and religious beliefs, Corinthians clung to an insidious skepticism. They doubted whether Jesus actually rose from the dead. A deceptive heresy existed that deserves attention.

Earlier in this letter, Paul confronted an attitude that continues to pervade Christian thinking. The problematic belief assumed that Christians receive the fullness of their inheritance in Christ immediately through baptism. Because baptism signified incorporation into the community of God, some of the Corinthian congregation believed they already had everything God promised them. To this Paul said, "Already you have all you

Resurrection was an already-complete event with no further implication or demand? that there was nothing much further to anticipate in living the life of Christ?

Read 1 Corinthians 15:12-19. Imagine that you are a member of the congregation at Corinth. You come from a Platonistic background and are aware of these other philosophies. You have accepted Jesus Christ as Savior because it seemed compatible with your existing beliefs about the immortality of the soul. Now you are being chided about the unity of body and soul and about how they tie into the resurrection of the body. What questions would you ask Paul? How do you feel about his sarcasm and his sense of urgency or impatience that you don't understand the way you should? What do you think you can anticipate later?

How do you understand "not yet-ness" and the ultimate things Paul is talking about? What would you ask him about it?

What happens to your spiritual motivation during times when you are forced to wait for some prayer request without any evidence that God will answer you soon?

want! Already you have become rich! You have become kings—and that without us! How I wish that you really had become kings, so that we might be kings with you!" (1 Corinthians 4:8, NIV). In other words, Is there nothing left to attain? Does God have nothing more beyond this earthly existence in store for us? These Corinthians demonstrated a kind of spiritual and religious arrogance that only warranted Paul's sarcasm.

While this line of thinking did not blatantly deny the resurrection of Christ, it affected their belief in the Resurrection. The logical end to this reasoning was to believe they already had in Christ all that they could expect in life. The danger of this approach to Christian discipleship was asserted in the claim of Hymenaeus and Philetus, that "the resurrection has already taken place" (2 Timothy 2:18).

Understandably, Paul referred to such a foolhardy notion as profane chatter to be avoided lest it spread like gangrene (2 Timothy 2:16-17). This "triumphant now" mentality failed to reconcile the tension between what one had already in Christ and what God promises as yet to come. Christ's resurrection paves the way for belief in our ultimate redemption in the general resurrection. For example, Paul spoke of God giving Christians the Holy Spirit as the pledge or down payment of what one can expect in fullness later (Ephesians 1:14). Scholar William Barclay's rendering of this passage clearly expresses the idea that having believed, you were marked in him with a seal, the promised Holy Spirit, who is a deposit guaranteeing our inheritance until the redemption of those who are God's possession. We have not received our full inheritance yet. Romans 8:22 tells us that all of creation is groaning in labor pains, in anticipation of what God has in store for us.

Paul's Unswerving Belief

Paul could argue confidently for belief in Christ's resurrection primarily because of his personal conversion experience. Prior to his Christian conversion, Paul's reputation was firmly established. Before meeting Christ, he was Saul of Tarsus, the Pharisee, the Roman citizen, the persecutor of the church. Only the extraordinary appearance of Christ could have uprooted his deeply embedded antagonism against the church.

On the road to Damascus, Paul experienced an undeniable encounter with the risen Christ. "He appeared *to me*," you can imagine him saying. "I experienced his life-changing power. I received this gospel message directly from the Lord himself." Paul was a personal witness of the risen Lord. He was proof positive of the transforming power of the gospel message; for him, there could be no reason for dispute.

We can perpetuate the reality of Christ's resurrection by sharing our testimony. Like Paul, many people have dramatic testimonies that demonstrate the ongoing power of the risen Christ. Each time we bear witness that Christ has transformed our lives, we share the power of Christ's resurrection with others. The power of Christ's resurrection was a much needed message because of the paralyzing view of death that some held.

Prevailing Hebrew Beliefs About Death

The introduction of the judgment of death in Genesis begins the Hebrews' fearful view of this foe (Genesis 2:15-17; 3:3-19). Hebrews first understood the flesh to be frail and weak as compared with the strength and

Paul's Unswerving Belief ■

Generally the most compelling beliefs or convictions are the result of firsthand experience, the "seeing is believing" approach. What is the most meaningful encounter that you have had with the Lord? In what ways has that encounter affected your life?

How does your understanding of eternal life influence the way you currently approach life? How does the way you approach life influence what you think and believe about eternal life? Do you think someone observing your life would come to the same conclusions as you have about eternal life or about Christian faith? Why or why not?

Bible 301 ☐

Look up several hymns about eternal life, assurance, or conviction. Sing or say some of them aloud. How do the words and music serve to convince you of the theology of God's continued presence with us in this life and in the next?

Beliefs About Death ■

Review the main points to be sure you understand the Hebrew beliefs about body, spirit/soul, and afterlife. What is *ruach*?

Read 1 Corinthians 15:20-26. Paul juxtaposes and contrasts Adam, the first person, and the first human to die because of sin, with Jesus Christ, the "new" Adam who, through his own death and resurrection, made "all alive." Study this passage by listing in one column the ways in which Adam is characterized and in another column the ways Jesus Christ is characterized. How does this comparison and explanation help the Corinthians understand Paul's argument? How does it help you?

How do you understand the language about "first fruits"?

In the Old Testament, when a person sensed that God's Spirit (*ruach*) was departing, they recognized the loss of vitality and powerlessness as a type of death. Share times when you have encountered a "deathly" experience. What types of thoughts and concerns have crossed your mind during these experiences?

Bible 301 ☐

Look up Sheol, Gehenna, *or* hell *in a Bible dictionary for more information about this place of afterlife. What is it? What happened to people there? How is it connected (or not) with the presence of God? How has the function and identity of*

power of God the Creator. Tragically, this fragile flesh was hopelessly separated from God. Despite this lowly state, humanity was clearly different, greater than the rest of God's creatures.

According to Hebrew belief, God infused humanity and all living things with *ruach* or God's Spirit. *Ruach* refers to the hidden strength of the living self. It is God's invasive power and ultimately belongs to God. Without the presence of this Spirit, a living being had no life, no vitality, and was, in effect, dead.

Adam was a living being into whom God had breathed life and in whom God was invested. As a creature of the flesh, though, the loss of breath in particular as well as the loss of blood (regarded as the source of life) were clear signs that this God-imparted life was departing. With these facts in mind, the careful description of Jesus' death on the cross is all the more significant. "Then Jesus gave a loud cry and *breathed his last*" (Mark 15:37, italics added). "Instead, one of the soldiers pierced his side with a spear and at once *blood and water came out*" (John 19:34, italics added). Clearly, the Gospel writers included these details to indicate that Jesus had indeed died.

Of interest to us is the Old Testament belief regarding what happens at the point of death and beyond. For the Jew, death meant that God withdrew God's Spirit (*ruach*) from one's house of flesh. The flesh then disintegrated while the essence of the person continued to exist beyond the reach of this world in *Sheol*—the dwelling place of the dead.

The prevailing understanding during the Old Testament was that the dead were powerless. Beyond this life, Hebrews believed that the dead existed in some obscure,

Sheol changed as the theology of Hebrew tradition has evolved?

Read Numbers 16:30; Job 10:21-22; Ephesians 4:8-10 for other biblical attributions of what *Sheol* or afterlife was. *Sheol* represented a place far removed from God's reign. Describe a *Sheol* experience that you have had. What kind of comfort would you have appreciated during that experience?

Beyond the loss of physical vitality, name ways in which people experience powerlessness. If we truly believe in the power of the Resurrection message, what can we do individually as Christians and collectively as a church to "resurrect" people from powerless conditions in your local area?

What Now?

At this point in your study of resurrection, what do you understand about how Jesus Christ has conquered death and provided for eternal life?

pathetic form, feeble and insubstantial, a ghostly reflection of their former selves. In this pitiable form, the dead traveled to the dark chaotic place of *Sheol*, which lay between the foundations of the earth (Numbers 16:30; Job 10:21-22).

This dwelling place of the dead was full of empty silence, a realm of no return. It represented separation from praise and remembrance of God. To be in *Sheol* was to be removed as far as possible from God's reign. Gradually, Hebrew thought developed that *Sheol* was accessible to God's power and rule (Psalm 139:8). It is this belief that conceivably paves the way for understanding Paul's teaching that Jesus descended into the abode of the living dead and released those who were captive (Ephesians 4:8-10).

Against this understanding of death's power to debilitate and banish a person to *Sheol*, Paul preached the good news. Faith in the resurrection of Christ brings deliverance from the dismal existence in *Sheol*. Confidently, Paul assured the Christians at Corinth that Christ is the Victor over every earthly power—including death. "The last enemy to be destroyed is death" (1 Corinthians 15:26).

What Now?

What do you mean, Paul? we may question. *People are still dying. Death does not seem to be conquered.* Paul was referring to the ultimate work of Christ when a new heaven and earth would come into existence. We now live in anticipation of Christ's second coming, which marks the final destruction of every rule, authority, and power that opposes the reign of God. Only then will death fold its hands and bow in complete submission (see Revelation 21:1). Currently, in our yet-to-beredeemed world, death continues to reign over our physical bodies until Christ ultimately destroys it and casts it into the lake of fire (Revelation 20:14). Someone may continue to press asking, But what about now? What good news do we have concerning death presently?

Hope in the Midst of Death

Take some quiet time either alone or with one other person to journal or tell about some of your experiences with death. Recall the death of someone who touched you. Remember the funeral or memorial service. What **theological message** was conveyed in spoken words, hymns, or liturgy? (These could be comments such as, "The Lord took him/her to a better place"; "She is with the angels"; "Now there is no more suffering with God"; "Nothing can separate us from the love of God"; and so on.) What did you find helpful? comforting? hopeful? What was theologically confusing or unhelpful?

Now recall the **pastoral (personal) messages** conveyed. What did you find helpful? comforting? hopeful? unhelpful?

Dealing with death is hard enough when we do believe in the Resurrection. How might you approach a

Hope in the Midst of Death

I have been with many Christian families visiting their loved ones in elder-care facilities. I have also accompanied parents visiting children in hospital intensive care units. When a disease or injuries from an accident, mercilessly pull on the last ounce of life, I have watched people find refuge in their faith in the Resurrection.

When the time comes to decide whether to sign "Do Not Resuscitate" papers, many families prayerfully concede that the physical body of their loved one will die. Then, however, they participate in a powerful act of faith. Somehow, with a sense of hopeful relief, they gather the courage to release their loved ones to pass through death and be with the Lord. Yes, they grieve losing the physical presence of that person. Yes, they mourn the loss of their companionship. But, there is no fear of that person passing into some powerless, shadowy existence, disconnected from God. No, their comfort is in knowing that beyond the reach of death, God is ready to receive the soul of their beloved and release them from the prison of this earthly body. Death does not have the final say.

With unflinching boldness, Paul pronounced the end to death's reign of terror as

grieving person who does not know Christ (because he or she is unchurched) or who is of another, non-Christian religion?

humanity's unconquerable foe. By the time Paul wrote Second Corinthians, he expressed a fearless attitude toward death: "Yes, we do have confidence, and we would rather be away from the body and at home with the Lord" (2 Corinthians 5:8). What better news could he share with the Jews who understood death as such a formidable foe? What better news could we hear when death taunts us with its temporary threats?

The Power of Resilience ■
The Power of Resurrection ■

(It would be helpful to study these Scriptures with added information from a Bible commentary.)

Read 1 Kings 17:17-24 and 2 Kings 4:17-37, the stories of miracles performed by Elijah and Elisha. What happened? What did the prophet do? Under what circumstances was he asked or brought to do it? What was the result? Now read John 11:1-44, the story of the raising of Lazarus. What are the differences in these stories? the similarities? Then compare all of them to the resurrection of Jesus. What is distinctly different about the resurrection of Jesus? If the healings of the children and Lazarus are resuscitations and not resurrections, does that seem to make any difference to the importance of the story and what it reveals about God's care and compassion? In any case, all three and the Resurrection are reported as miracles or signs of

The Power of Christ's Resurrection

We experience the dynamic power of Christ's resurrection when we identify the basic message of the gospel of Jesus Christ. Paul spelled out the fundamental message of the gospel for us— Christ died for our sins, was buried, and was raised on the third day. Each part of this message carries clear implications. Paul mentioned that Jesus was buried in order to underscore the reality that Christ actually died. He did not go into a coma. Christ endured tortuous beatings and exposure on the cross. After he breathed his last, a soldier pierced him in the side. The separation of blood and water demonstrated that he was dead.

Thankfully, Jesus accomplished something in his death; he paid the penalty for our sin. His death reveals the tremendous love that God has for us in sending Christ to die in our place.

Last, the gospel message states that Christ was raised from the dead in accordance with the Scriptures. Some will argue that Jesus' resurrection was not the first. Elijah revived a boy (1 Kings 17:21-22) and so did Elisha (2 Kings 4:34-35). Jesus restored Lazarus from the dead (John 11:43-45). Were these instances of resurrection or resuscitation? Certainly, these miracles returned the individual's life, but they all eventually died again.

God's power and concern for humankind. How do they illuminate the idea of resurrection and hope for the future?

By contrast, Jesus was resurrected from the dead to live forever. That is, he returned to experience life differently. His form had changed. Christ appeared to Paul, the disciples, and the five hundred witnesses in an eternal glorified body (1 Corinthians 15:3-8). Jesus' resurrection shows Christians that we can look forward to resurrection to a new life. We will have a new eternal existence with a new body. Resurrection is not the resuscitation of the old body.

Identifying with the power of Christ's resurrection can occur in practical ways. It represents hope in the face of hopelessness. As Christians, we are to persevere in our walk with Christ until he returns. In his message to the church in Philadelphia in Asia Minor, Jesus promised to reward them. "Because you have kept my word of patient endurance, I will keep you from the hour of trial that is coming on the whole world to test the inhabitants of the earth" (Revelation 3:10). Their belief in the risen Christ gave them inspiration to endure life's struggles. We can endure trials because we identify with Christ's resurrection and have hope in God.

New Beginnings ▪

Read Revelation 3:7-13, the words of the angel to the church in Philadelphia. What message does it convey to you? How is it a message of hope (and warning) to the church?

New Beginnings

Christ's resurrection symbolizes new beginnings. Jesus promised a New Jerusalem: "If you conquer, I will make you a pillar in the temple of my God; you will never go out of it. I will write on you the name of my God, and the name of the city of my God, the new Jerusalem that comes down from my God out of heaven, and my own new name" (Revelation 3:12).

The disciples had constantly been longing for Christ to establish the New Jerusalem. Just before Christ ascended, they asked him, "Lord, is this the time when you will restore

Close With Prayer

Identify other areas of your life that need hope, such as attitudes, behaviors, practices, and so on. Offer these areas to God during your regular prayer and devotional times.

Ask for prayer requests from the group. Are there areas in your own life that seem hopeless? Pray for the power of Christ's resurrection to restore your hope.

After praying for these specific requests, join together in the following prayer:

Dear Lord, the simple gospel message indicates that we must die in order to receive new life. Show each of us those attitudes, behaviors, and thoughts that need to die in order for new life to emerge. Strengthen our faith and trust in you through regular encounters with your holy presence. Rekindle our dying hopes and clarify our understanding of the basic gospel message that Christ died, was buried, and was raised for our salvation. For the dead and powerless areas of our lives, bring resurrection. Help us to experience the power of the Resurrection in our daily lives. Thank you for sacrificing your life so that we may experience new life; we pray in Jesus' name. Amen.

the kingdom to Israel?" (Acts 1:6). We are nearer the restoration of God's kingdom than ever before. The New Jerusalem represents a new beginning. It is a time when God's reign will be in effect throughout the world.

We can establish new beginnings each day by forgiving others and giving them a new start. We can forgive ourselves for past failures and start a new day. We can carry the message of Christ to people without faith and give them new hope. With Christ, we can restore our run-down neighborhoods. Through the power of Christ's resurrection, all things can become new.

We can take comfort in knowing that the resurrected Christ conquered death. Through Jesus Christ, we have access to new life, a life that transcends the limited confines dictated by these earthly bodies. We can be assured of the reality of the Resurrection because the living Christ is the proof that God can resurrect the dead. As Christians, we need not fear the grave and beyond. Paul's triumphal statement is worth repeating here. "Death has been swallowed up in victory. / Where, O death, is your victory? / Where, O death, is your sting? (1 Corinthians 15:54b-55).

Session Seven

A New Type of Existence, A New Type of Body

Session Focus ■

Living eternally with God requires a new resurrected body fit for spiritual purposes. As we live in anticipation of receiving this new body, we have an earthly task. Christianity requires that we put this sinful nature to death in order to participate in Christian living.

Session Objective ■

Through this study we will explore the practical process of experiencing new life through Christ.

Session Preparation ■

Prepare index cards. Have on hand a recording of Handel's *Messiah,* specifically the section, "The Trumpet Shall Sound," for a *Bible 301* activity and a tape or CD player.

Choose from among these activities and discussion starters to plan your lesson.

1 Corinthians 15:35-58

In the twentieth century, we simply dyed gray hair or tried a new fitness program to ward off aging. In this new millennium, we have the technology to be more advanced than that. Will medical science offer us cloned replacement parts to extend our lives indefinitely? Will we disconnect genes responsible for aging?

Why do we fear death? Despite the protectiveness we have toward our bodies, Paul insisted that this body must die in order to receive a new resurrected body. What did Paul mean? This chapter compels us to search for answers to crucial questions. To find answers however, we often begin with more questions.

What kind of body will we have in the resurrection? This is a question that plagues the minds of people today just as it did in Paul's time. Trying to understand the various aspects of resurrection is like trying to navigate uncharted waters without a compass. There is good reason for such uncertainty because the resurrection event is what scholars refer to as a *novum*—a new, unexpected act of God that has no precedent in history.

You recall from the previous chapter, that miraculous revivals had occurred before; but never had someone died and been raised to a new type of existence in a new type of body. God injected this never-before-conceived reality into our finite human world. Now we are confronted with the task of understanding this new body and this new existence offered through Christ's resurrection. Paul begins to address this phenomenon in 1 Corinthians 15:35.

Death and the Resurrected Body ■

Divide 1 Corinthians 15:35-58 among three groups (verses 35-41; 42-49; 50-58). Do not try to examine the text closely yet, but list all of the images and metaphors Paul uses to make his point. Write key terms on poster paper or a chalkboard so they can be prominently displayed during the lesson. As you work through the lesson, jot down brief definitions or explanations of what those metaphors refer to and how they are used.

Death and the Resurrected Body

Paul explodes with exasperation, calling foolish those who considered themselves "wise": "Fool! What you sow does not come to life unless it dies" (1 Corinthians 15:36). Earlier in this chapter, we experienced a taste of Paul's challenge. The verbal jab "Fool!" here refers to someone who is foolish in spiritual matters. How could Paul help them understand the nature of the resurrection body they were to receive through Christ?

Even in a commercial center like Corinth, concrete agricultural examples proved to be a most effective means of communicating spiritual concepts, especially when he was addressing the issue on two levels. Paul used the imagery of a seed sown into the earth to demonstrate his point. A seed bears no resemblance to what it will ultimately become. An apple seed is very different from an apple tree. So it is with our earthly bodies. Our present bodies are different from the resurrected body that we will receive. Most assuredly however, the first step in this process involves dying.

Paul refers to the Corinthian Christians as spiritually foolish. Since spiritual wisdom comes from the Holy Spirit's instruction, share practical ways in which we can actively seek the guidance of the Holy Spirit.

Paul continues with simple logic. In order to experience the resurrection, what we were previously must die. Death is not an obstacle to resurrection; it is a necessary part of the process. People still struggle with the inevitability of death. Paul insists that death will occur. These bodies are weak and perishable. They will die. As Paul's argument unfolds, we see that he is referring to changes that occur in this life to reform and transform this life (a "little" death), while in the main he is expanding on a transcendant level about physical death and eternal life.

A New Kind of Body

A New Kind of Body ■

Some Corinthians had adopted the Greek belief that considered the body and all physical matter to be evil. *How could God glorify what many people considered to be evil and unredeemable?* they thought. Paul responded that each type of body that God created is glorious, but each one is created to serve a different function. "God gives it a body as he has chosen, and to each kind of seed its own body. Not all flesh is alike . . ." (15:38-39a).

God fashioned humankind to serve a specific function. We were created to glorify God. No matter how gloriously we function in this body however, these fragile bodies are not fit to glorify God eternally. We shall all be changed. This addresses the fears of people who wonder how they can live eternally with a body that has been mangled in an accident or ravaged by a deadly disease.

Beginning with verse 42, Paul makes the distinction between our present physical bodies and our coming spiritual bodies: "The body that is sown is perishable, it is raised imperishable; . . . it is sown a natural body, it is raised a spiritual body" (15:42b, 44a, NIV). Here Paul employs a typical tactic of using terms and images that sound familiar to a Platonic mindset (which divides the body and spirit, where Hebrew thought does not). Platonic philosophy would never understand the resurrection of a physical or natural body. Paul's task was to assert that there will be a

Sidebar:

Look more closely at 1 Corinthians 15:39-44. How are the terms *flesh, seed, perishable,* and *imperishable* used here?

Paul distinguishes between the bodies of persons and of various animals, but they are all perishable. Is Paul suggesting that the perishable bodies of animals are somehow raised to an imperishable form? If not, what is the point of mentioning them? How does this image fit his analogy?

How is God's glory described? How does this fit Paul's understanding of what is raised?

The Greeks believed that

all matter, including the body, was evil. What problems can arise from such a view of the body? Paul describes our physical bodies as perishable and subject to earthly desires. With this in mind, how is it possible for our bodies to be employed for spiritual purposes?

general resurrection of the body; but in the resurrected life, the body would not be physical. It would be changed. By the end of the chapter, Paul bluntly states that "flesh and blood cannot inherit the kingdom of God" (15:50b).

What major changes do you believe will occur as you participate more and more in your new life in Christ?

Sarx and Soma

Paul employs two Greek terms in his argument about resurrection of the body to blend Greek philosophy and Hebrew psychology. Sarx generally refers to the body physically as bones and tissues, and it is the sarx (one's carnal nature) that is heir to sin.

In contrast, the soma *is the spiritual body; those familiar with Platonic philosophy would consider it separate and distinct from the sarx. Paul asserted that there must be both. The unity of body, mind, soul, and spirit was the soma, and this was what gave each person a distinct personality and uniqueness.*

So, what happens when we die? Paul melds the concept of the resurrection of the soma with the Greek concept of the immortality of the soul. Sarx will perish because it is made of mortal flesh, but the essence of the individual—soma— will exist eternally. In that way, "we will bear the image of the man of heaven" (15:49).

The Death of the Flesh

Read 1 Corinthians 15:45-49, Paul's comments about Adam and the "second man." Who is the "second man"? How is he contrasted with the first man?

The Death of the Flesh

When Paul speaks of the death process, he is stating that our physical bodies are unsuitable for eternity because they are perishable. They are also unsuitable for spiritual service because of the old sinful Adamic nature. We are earthly creatures like Adam was. Some commentaries use the term *fleshly body*. In the

Paul says that Jesus Christ, the second man, atones for and makes right the unrighteousness or sin of the first man, Adam. Adam is a "type," something that would be familiar in Platonic reasoning. In this sense, then, Adam is an "everyperson" who repre- sents the fall from perfec- tion, grace, and eternity that God apparently intend- ed in the Garden.

Read Genesis 2:8-9, 15- 17; 3:1-24. This passage presents the first nature and the fallen nature. What are they? How does Paul use this story to help make his point about the ulti- mate life that God intends?

New Testament, when writers used the terms *fleshly body*, or *the flesh*, *(sarx)* they were com- monly referring to the sinful element of human nature, but Paul also used the word *flesh* to refer to the physical body that would decay after burial. Keeping track of which meaning Paul is using, especially when he can intend both meanings, can be confusing.

In our previous chapter, we explored some of the concerns that we hold about physical death. Now, our focus shifts to the process of putting our old nature "to death," that is, being transformed in this life to an orienta- tion to Christ. Why must this "flesh" die? The answer is simple. The flesh, our old sin- ful nature, is the essence of selfishness. It cannot do spiritual things. Without Christ, our human nature is driven to pursue the satisfaction of our worldly appetites. *I, me,* and *mine* are our primary concern. We are speaking of what Paul calls corruptible or perishable seed (see also 1 Peter 1:23). The core of the flesh is sinful. We discover this the moment we begin to follow the path of Christianity.

We are created as soma—a unity of body, mind, spirit, and soul, but likewise prone to sin. This sinful nature is not destroyed at sal- vation. A life lived in Christ transforms our nature toward godliness. But, we must still contend with the warring of these two natures.

Spiritual Tension

Have you noticed how as Christians we attempt to pay careful attention to what we should or shouldn't do? The rationale begins, "If I can simply correct a few bad behaviors, then I will be a good Christian." We try to be kind, but unchecked anger still lashes out. We try to love everyone, but old

Spiritual Tension ■

Ask volunteers from the group to share briefly any frustrations that they remember facing as new Christians. In what ways should Christians attempt to subdue the problem of sin in their lives?

From your observations, how well do Christians overcome personal sin? In dealing with sin, do you believe it is more effective to concentrate on stopping the sinful act or determining its root cause?

Discuss any personal challenges involved with relinquishing control over your life.

prejudices inspire us to spew hateful remarks. We simply cannot keep our old human nature in check. We try to please God, but something within us resists. *Why can't I stop doing wrong*, we wonder? The problem is not first what we do outwardly, it is what we *are* inwardly.

Paul experienced this spiritual tension himself. "For what I do is not the good I want to do; no, the evil I do not want to do—this I keep on doing. Now if I do what I do not want to do, it is no longer I who do it, but it is sin living in me that does it. . . . What a wretched man I am! Who will rescue me from this body of death?" (Romans 7:19-20, 24, NIV). Paul is bemoaning the continued activity of his old nature that we must discard. But how do we discard it?

A Life of Godlinesss

Read Romans 7:14–8:17 and 1 Corinthians 15:56-58—passages that reflect on how God gives humankind the power to resist sin through the work of Jesus Christ and the Holy Spirit. What do these Scriptures suggest to you about being "rescued from this body of death"? Can you open yourself to allow this godly working in you?

A Life of Godliness

Paul answered his own question: "Thanks be to God through Jesus Christ—our Lord! ... There is now no condemnation for those who are in Christ Jesus. For the law of the Spirit of life in Christ Jesus has set you free from the law of sin and of death" (7:25a, 8:1-2). Paul goes on to point out that "to set the mind on the flesh is death, but to set the mind on the Spirit is life and peace" (8:6).

Paul pursues the same line of reasoning in his Letter to the Corinthians and concludes with these words of encouragement: "Therefore, my beloved, be steadfast, immovable, always excelling in the work of the Lord, because you know that in the Lord your labor is not in vain" (1 Corinthians 15:56-58).

The New Life

The idea of crucifying the flesh is a radically transforming act. Do you see

Taking on the New Life

When we believe by faith that Christ died for us, we become participants in his death on the cross. To experience the reality of this dying process as essential to your Christian walk? What does being crucified with Christ mean to you?

What advice would you share with someone who professes Christ as Lord yet refuses to participate in the process of self-denial?

Review again what is meant by the two natures.

Paul, in another letter, uses the metaphor of clothing to speak about putting off the old (earthly) life and putting on the new (in the image of its creator). He refers to the physical life, but it serves the Kingdom.

In two teams, read Colossians 3:5-8; 3:12-17. On index cards, write out the vices and the virtues, one to a card. Distribute the cards, one to a person (make more than one copy of the cards for a large group). Then pair up, having one of the virtues cover one of the vices. In those pairs, identify examples in daily life that fit the vice and then examples of the virtue that can correct the vice. For example, a daily instance of anger is losing one's temper with a fellow employee before finding out the facts; a corrective example of the virtue of patience is taking time to find out what there is to know before speaking and acting.

dying with Christ, we must pronounce the death of our former "self-directed life." Like Paul, in his agonizing over evil and good behavior, we commit to ongoing vigilance against the behaviors that break down and destroy. The new life in Christ is a life that the Spirit of God controls. This new life causes us to rethink the way that we conduct our lives. As we intentionally "crucify" our old nature, we relinquish the right to control and manipulate the new life we have in Jesus Christ. This new way of living is a mere foretaste of the new existence we will experience in our resurrected bodies.

Christ's teachings about the kingdom of God demands this commitment. Love your enemy. If you are compelled by a Roman soldier to walk a mile, offer to walk two miles. If you are struck on the cheek, offer the other (see Matthew 5–7). Paul phrases these ethical demands in another way. "Put to death, therefore, whatever in you is earthly: fornication, impurity, passion, evil desire, and greed" (Colossians 3:5). How can a person do such things?

This "death" process involves a radical transformation of our human will. As we allow the Holy Spirit to direct our lives, we learn to put the old life in the past. As Paul stated in another letter: "These are the ways you also once followed, when you were living that life. But now you must get rid of all such things. . . . As God's chosen ones, holy and beloved, clothe yourselves with compassion, kindness, humility, meekness, and patience. Bear with one another and, if anyone has a complaint against another, forgive each other; just as the Lord has forgiven you, so you also must forgive" (Colossians 3:7-8a, 12-13). As we willingly participate with God in this dramatic process, we begin to live as those crucified with Christ and raised to new life through Christ.

Accepting the Mystery of God

Before closing, Paul speaks of a great mystery in the new life to come, "We will not all die, but we will all be changed, in a moment, in the twinkling of an eye, at the last trumpet" (1 Corinthians 15:51b-52a). Paul and many first-century Christians lived with the anticipation of Christ's second coming within their lifetime. Not everyone will have to experience physical death. Enoch and Elijah point to this reality (Genesis 5:24; 2 Kings 2:11). Both entered into God's presence without tasting death. When Christ returns again, Christians' bodies will be transformed in an instant. How? It's a mystery.

Every aspect of resurrection is a mystery. It confounds logic. It is humanly impossible to explain. The Resurrection itself was an unexpected act of God. It was a mystery, yet Paul spoke of it with the confidence and assurance of someone speaking about a well-established truth. Mystery lies at the core of the Christian faith.

Jesus Christ is 100 percent God *and* 100 percent man. How is that possible? It's a mystery. Crucify him; and three days later, God raises his body from the dead to live in a new mode of existence. How? It's a mystery. The Christian faith requires us to acknowledge the unfathomable vastness of God, a vastness so expansive that we can never comprehend all there is to know about God. It is at this point that God's mystery is revealed. *How* God brings about the Incarnation and the Resurrection are unknown to us, but to see *what* and *who* God is, we need only look to the Son. For Paul and for us, this is enough.

Fourth-century desert father, Abba

Accepting the Mystery of God

Read 1 Corinthians 15:50-58. How would you describe a theological or spiritual mystery (with greater depth than "we don't know")?

The mystery of God escapes many of our probing inquiries. How difficult is it for you to live with unanswered questions about God and the Christian faith?

How do you reconcile any tensions caused by spiritual ambiguities?

Bible 301 ☐

If possible, play a recording of 1 Corinthians 15:52—"The Trumpet Shall Sound" from Handel's Messiah. Is there something about hearing this passage set to music that makes the message more accessible or understandable?

Explore the idea of victory over death: the result of the mortal body "putting on" imperishability. How do you understand this victory?

Briefly tell stories or journal about an experience in which death was "swallowed up in victory." This concept doesn't seem strange for someone who believes in resurrection and eternal life, especially in a death that is "timely." How can an untimely death "lose its sting" or be "swallowed up in victory"?

Explore the image of a "relaxed heart." How does your knowledge of the old and new natures and the promise of resurrection "gentle" your heart to make space for God?

How do you best converse with God? How does this method of conversation turn you around and make you more aware of the mysteries of God?

Pambo, said, "Acquire a heart and you shall be saved." For the desert fathers, the focus of prayer and other spiritual disciplines was to acquire a purity of heart that rendered a person "permeable" and available to God's mystery. A heart permeable to God and God's mystery lowers its defenses, becomes compassionate, allows God's love and grace to flow in, and learns to trust.

As with any other spiritual transformation, acquiring a permeable heart is a process that is possible only when we seek it intentionally. Instead of trying to force the mystery of God to exhibit a more "recognizable and understandable" form, our efforts may be better spent seeking a change of mind. We speak here of a change of purpose, a transformation, or what French writer André Louf describes as a "relaxation of heart" that allows the heart to be "gentled" in such a way as to make space for God.

Along this spiritual journey, repentance becomes a necessary theme repeated throughout our lifetimes. Accepting the mystery of God requires a view of repentance that turns away from a stubborn, obstinate position that cannot accept what is new, different, and unexplainable. Conversation and conversion come from the same Latin root—*conversare*, meaning "to turn around." In its passive form it becomes "to be turned around." Our ability to embrace the mystery of God can only be developed through regular conversation with the Living Word, and our lives are transformed when we allow God to turn us around.

The more we converse with God, the more our lives get turned around spiritually. The more we converse with God, the more we learn to be shaped by God's perspective and agree to God's leading. God will forever create new unexplainable things that have no precedent. If we can accept the mystery of God as "normal," then we can accept the mystery of the Resurrection.

Contemporary Considerations

Paul's message to the Corinthians exposes his raw passion for proclaiming the basic gospel message—Christ died, was buried, and was raised from the dead. For him and for us, this is the cornerstone of our Christian faith. Christ's resurrection ushers in a new reality, a new hope for what lies beyond this life, and a new challenge to believe in the mystery of God.

God should remain beyond the reach of our well-crafted categories. God would not be God if God only did what *we* expected and remained within the confines of *our* reality. God stands just beyond the reach of objective inquiry but well within the range of faith. Open your heart, converse with the living Word, and make room for the mystery of God.

As we learn to trust God, mystery and all, we begin to learn how to experience new life in Christ. We can actively participate in this new existence by crucifying our old selves and placing control of our new lives into God's hands. Our lives and deeds belong to God. "Therefore, my beloved, be steadfast, immovable, always excelling in the work of the Lord, because you know that in the Lord your labor is not in vain" (1 Corinthians 15:58). There is no greater joy than experiencing new life in Christ and anticipating our new glorified bodies in the Resurrection.

Contemporary Considerations ■

Summarize your understandings of the new type of existence and the new type of body. What is it that helps you to "be steadfast, immovable, always excelling in the work of the Lord" (1 Corinthians 15:58)?

Close With Prayer ■

Silently pray for God to show you how to put your self-directed life to death. Ask for prayer requests. Incorporate them in the following prayer:

Dear Lord, we are beginning to understand your desire for us to participate in the new life available through Jesus Christ. Help us to accept that putting our selfish natures to death is part of the process of experiencing new life. Lead us to discover the joy of leading a Spirit-directed life. Send your resurrection power to renew our lives now. Amen.

Session Eight

Finishing Touches

Session Focus ■

This lesson focuses primarily on the Ascension and the Great Commission. A general summary of the book concludes the chapter.

Session Objective ■

The aim of this session is to stimulate thoughtful consideration of how one should carry out the Great Commission.

Session Preparation ■

Have on hand a Bible dictionary, a commentary on Galatians, copies of your hymnal or book of worship, and a Bible atlas to do the *Bible 301* activities.

Choose from among these activities and discussion starters to plan your lesson.

Matthew 28:16-20; Acts 1:1-11

Christ lived, Christ died, Christ rose from the dead—what does this mean for us practically? Because of Christ's crucifixion and resurrection, salvation is available to us. With salvation comes Christ's challenging command—the Great Commission. As Christians, we are the Lord's ambassadors on earth, empowered by the Holy Spirit to share the good news of Jesus Christ *with the world*. Let that sink in.

By his death and resurrection, Jesus Christ received complete power over the universe from God. Through his disciples, Christ then initiated a universal mission—the Great Commission. The universal sovereignty of the risen Lord dominates the closing scene in Matthew. In Acts 1, the message of Christ's ascension continues to stress the Lord's universal sovereignty and power. The Ascension further emphasized that Jesus transferred the gospel mission into the disciples' hands. With the Ascension, Christ's work of atonement was complete. The ascended Lord now sits in glory on the right hand of the throne of Majesty in heaven. From this honored position, Jesus as High Priest and King sends the Holy Spirit. This Great Commission now comes to us from the ascended Christ, who has all power and all authority.

The Great Commission

Read Matthew 28:16-20. Check out the verbs. What does Jesus ask all disciples to do?

Share your responses to the idea that the church is a "go" structure rather than a "come" structure. Is your church set up as a "go" or a "come" structure or a blend of both? How do you participate in the going and coming functions of your church?

Read Matthew 10:5-6. What possible reasons might Jesus have had for placing this limitation on the disciples' ministry at this time?
What personal obstacles did the apostles face when they had to minister outside of the house of Israel? Now that much of the US looks like a small United Nations in its diversity, what obstacles do we face in terms of spreading the gospel?

Carrying Out the Great Commission

When Jesus appeared to the eleven disciples on a mountain in Galilee, he charged them to "go" and "make" disciples (Matthew 28:16-20). I remember a preacher saying, the church is a "go structure" not a "come structure." With that pointed statement, he was trying to move the congregation beyond the four walls of the church building. The church is a living, breathing organism that survives through multiplication. It is true that Christians should "come" together for worship, spiritual nurture, education, and fellowship; but the Great Commission clearly indicates that the Lord expects the church to "go" to people and share Christ.

Jesus' charge for the disciples to go to all peoples was a radical change for them. Matthew records that up to this point, their religious focus had been the house of Israel. During his earthly ministry, Jesus echoed this sentiment. Before sending the twelve disciples out to cure the sick and cast out demons, he gave them the following instructions: "Go nowhere among the Gentiles, and enter no town of the Samaritans, but go rather to the lost sheep of the house of Israel" (Matthew 10:5-6). Following Jesus' resurrection, Matthew's Gospel promotes a universal appeal. For the first time, the disciples are to share Christ's teachings with *everybody*.

Following his resurrection, Christ emphasized that the gospel message is a universal message. The gospel message is designed to remove the barriers of separation between peoples. Paul strongly reaffirms this idea in Romans by borrowing from the prophet Joel. There he writes, "For there is no distinction between Jew and Greek; the same Lord is Lord of all and is generous to all who call on

Examine an "off limits" ministry. Read Matthew 9:10-11 and John 4:9, 27a and enough of the surrounding text to understand what was going on. What are the issues and concerns raised in these situations? Who is "off limits" and why? What did it mean for Jesus to break the barriers and act, regardless of the controversy it created?

How do we establish what is off limits regarding our socializing, choice of residence, choice of vocation, locale of work or school, and so on? Are these barriers mirrored by your church? by its location? by its members or ministry? Our churches are usually the most homogeneous organizations in which we participate. What does this say about our intention to "go to all nations"?

A Word of Caution

Do you think Christians are called to go everywhere? Does Christianity have a right to assert its authority in places that are primarily non-Christian? Explain.

Read Acts 10:1-48. Do this as a dramatic reading with volunteers taking the part of Peter, a narrator,

him. For, 'Everyone who calls on the name of the Lord shall be saved' " (Romans 10:12-13; see also Joel 2:23). Harmful exclusions of ethnic groups must disappear when we share the gospel message. As America becomes more ethnically diverse, the relevance of the Great Commission becomes more apparent. We do not have to go very far to reach "all nations" anymore.

Jesus was not asking the disciples to do anything that he had not already modeled, however. Throughout his earthly ministry, Jesus ate with, spoke to, and ministered among people whom the Jews considered "off limits." He ministered to people the Pharisees despised. "And as he sat at dinner in the house, many tax collectors and sinners came and were sitting with him and his disciples. When the Pharisees saw this, they said to his disciples, 'Why does your teacher eat with tax collectors and sinners?' " (Matthew 9:10-11). He also ministered to people the disciples would have avoided. "The Samaritan woman said to him, 'How is it that you, a Jew, ask a drink of me, a woman of Samaria?' (Jews do not share things in common with Samaritans.) . . . Just then his disciples came. They were astonished that he was speaking with a woman" (John 4:9, 27a).

A Word of Caution

Some commentators offer a word of caution to us before we gear up to "go" into "all the world." First, we need to assess our level of acceptance of other people. Are all Christians called to go everywhere? This is a question for us to consider very carefully. Peter struggled with his strong sense of Jewish nationalism, but he came to embrace his mission to the Gentiles with great openness (Acts 10:1-48). When sent by a godly

Cornelius, and the godly messengers. Try to illustrate verbally the change of heart and mind Peter experienced in taking up this ministry to a Gentile territory and household.

Then read Galatians 2:11-14. What was the fuss about? Missionary activity to persons who are different carries its own risks and difficulties, if not with the receiving group, then possibly with the "home" group. How do we responsibly "go to other nations" without creating unnecessary tensions? (Is this an appropriate goal?) How did Paul address Peter's prejudice against the Gentiles? Who challenges you when you become biased?

Bible 301 ☐

Use a Bible commentary or dictionary to find out more about the "circumcision party." Why did Peter not want to alienate this group?

Taking Our Place ▪

In three groups, look at each of these suggestions for taking a place in God's great drama. Brainstorm ways that you personally could fulfill the option considered by your group.

vision to the home of the Gentile Cornelius, Peter could proclaim: "I truly understand that God shows no partiality, but in every nation anyone who fears him and does what is right is acceptable to him" (10:34-35).

Even with that transforming revelation, Peter at times fell back into "partial" behavior and was criticized by Paul. "But when Cephas [Peter] came to Antioch, I opposed him to his face, because he stood self-condemned; for until certain people came from James, he used to eat with the Gentiles. But after they came, he drew back and kept himself separate for fear of the circumcision faction" (Galatians 2:11-12). Evidently Peter felt that his association with Gentiles was proper but didn't want some of the Jews to know about it.

This word of caution does not release us from participating in the Great Commission, however. The call to overseas mission, urban ministry, and elsewhere remains in effect. Our first response to Christ's call is obedience. We must be willing to go wherever and do whatever the Lord directs. As Christ neared his ascension, he enlisted the disciples to assume responsibility for his universal mission of salvation on the earth. As baptized believers, we too share this responsibility. As the body of Christ, we are both the object of God's love and the agent of God's purpose.

Taking Our Place in God's Drama

Our task is to discern what specific role we should play in God's great drama. Here are some practical suggestions to get people started: (1) Tell the story of Christ. Simply share your personal relationship with Christ. (2) As inhabitants of one of the richest countries in the world, we need to share our

What are the barriers to ful-
filling the ideas you brainstormed? What would it
take to overcome them?
What other suggestions can
you think of that have not
been mentioned?

Share your reactions to the
idea of mission using military, colonial, or commercial metaphors. Are there
ways that we perpetuate
any of these inappropriate
models for mission today?
Consider the "tourist"
model. The group comes in
as a tourist, without taking
time to understand the culture; does its mission pro-
ject, regardless of how local
people feel about it; and
leaves with a "feel-good"
belief that it has made a
difference because the resi-
dents have a new front
porch or a new roof or new
clothes. What is right and
what is wrong with this
model?

wealth with others. (3) We can make friends across racial/ethnic or national boundaries. Establishing friendships provides wonderful opportunities to share Christ.

These suggestions may not seem overly dramatic or effective to those who see mission in a different light. In the past, the church has sometimes used military, colonial, and commercial metaphors in mission. There are pitfalls in trying to view missions in these ways.

Military metaphors imply that people need to be subdued, conquered, and defeated —for Christ. By contrast, Christ command-ed the Eleven to make disciples. The colonial metaphor suggests occupation, planta-tions, and the imposition of foreign culture to effect transformation among the natives. In actuality, the gospel should transform us. We and our culture should reflect Christ more readily. The commercial metaphor paints the world as a religious market full of potential customers of Christianity. Disciples of Christ become salespersons trying to per-suade people to try their product. We are then tempted to measure success primarily by the numbers of souls reached. Yet, the Bible teaches us that souls are won to God by our witness and the conviction of the Holy Spirit (John 17:6-8). As twenty-first-century Christians, we may need to rethink how we should carry out the Great Commission.

Go and Make Disciples

While the focus of the Great Commission is commonly on *going* to all nations, more attention may need to be given to *making* disciples. Matthew spent the greater part of twenty-eight chapters describing what it means to be a disciple of Christ. One com-

Go and Make Disciples

What specific role(s) do you
believe Christ has asked
you to play in carrying out
the Great Commission?
Write the names of at least
12 geographical locations

on slips of paper. Include some local, some national, and some international locations. Give each group member one of the slips of paper when they enter the room. Read Acts 1:8 and substitute the names of the geographical locations that you wrote on the slips of paper.

How would you express your feelings about carrying out Christ's commission in "your" assigned location? What information would you need first? What kind of education or training? How would you prepare? Who would you enlist for help?

What is involved in "making" disciples? How different might our approach to mission be if we focused mainly on making disciples?

Christian Baptism ■

Tell baptism stories. Since baptism is a corporate act, you have been a participant in every baptism you have witnessed as well as in your own baptism. What happened? Who was present? Who wore what clothes? Who took vows and what were they? What did the baptism mean to you?

Review the Scriptures in this section that refer to baptism. What are the different understandings of the purpose of baptism?

mentator concludes that the main verb in Matthew 28:19 is *make*, to which everything else is subordinate. Indeed, the lifelong process of becoming a disciple and teaching discipleship should be our greatest priority. Jesus' teaching focused on the drastic change in living required in the kingdom of God. The effectiveness of the Great Commission depends in part on our willingness to exhibit "Kingdom principles." Consider the impact we could make if we consistently carried out one of Jesus' teachings such as, "Love your enemies, do good to those who hate you, bless those who curse you, pray for those who abuse you" (Luke 6:27-28). When we decide to live the gospel, we share the gospel.

Religions in the first century were noted for expecting clear declarations of loyalty and allegiance. Christianity was no different. There needed to be a clear line of demarcation indicating that a person now belonged to Christ. Baptism became that sign.

The Significance of Christian Baptism

For the Jews, baptism was already an established practice. Jewish rules of purification were concerned with ritual uncleanness. From that background, baptism became associated with the idea of "purification" from all that might exclude a person from God's presence. Baptism was part of the requirement for Gentile proselytes seeking admission to Israel. For them, baptism symbolized religious, moral, and ritual cleansing from the defilement of paganism. John the Baptist placed a stronger emphasis on repentance. He also favored baptism along with acquiring a solid foundation of moral teaching (Luke 3:3, 10-14). For John the Baptist, baptism was initiation into a community preparing for the Messiah's coming (Luke 3:16-17).

What is the symbolism? Who can be baptized? Summarize the meaning of baptism from John the Baptist to Paul. What insights did you gain from your summary?

What does it mean to be baptized "in the name" of Jesus Christ? Matthew 28:19 requires a trinitarian formula: in the name of Father, Son, and Holy Spirit. What does this mean? What does it mean to you? Is it enough to be baptized in the name of Christ? Explain.

Bible 301 ☐

Using a Bible dictionary and other denominational resources, look further into the history, purpose, and method of baptism. Various denominations hold different theological stances and practices. United Methodists, for example, practice infant baptism and allow sprinkling, pouring, or immersing in water and theologically never permit rebaptism. Southern Baptists immerse persons in a believer's baptism. What does your church do and why?

Locate a baptismal liturgy from your hymnal or book

As the disciples carried out the Great Commission, the doctrine of baptism continued to develop. When the apostle Peter baptized in Acts 2:38-39, he also maintained that baptism included repentance, remission and washing away of sin, and admission to the religious community. In addition, he maintained that with Christian baptism one received the gift of the Holy Spirit. Baptism became the expected response to the gospel of Christ, the Savior.

When a person was baptized "in the name" or "into the name" of Jesus Christ, it indicated that he or she came under Christ's authority and protection. The baptized person was now personally committed to all of the privileges and obligations of the Christian life. The apostle Paul brought further depth and clarity to the doctrine of baptism. Paul added the idea of being "sealed" with the purchaser's mark; that is with Christ's Spirit (2 Corinthians 1:21-22).

As we consider the role of baptism in the life of contemporary Christianity, Paul's teaching bears reviewing. He insists that no one is saved by his or her own good works— not even the good work of baptism. We are saved only by faith in the risen Christ (Romans 3:20; 4:4-5; Galatians 3:2, 11). Perhaps the most relevant of Paul's teachings on baptism are those that tie its significance to the crucifixion and resurrection of Christ.

Paul assumes the original immersion method of baptism. The symbolism is clear; to be immersed in baptism is likened to being buried with Christ (Colossians 2:11-12). Being "in Christ" meant putting off the old sinful nature. In place of this "dead" person, a newly born individual arose renewed and transformed from the baptismal waters, just as Christ was raised from the grave. In

of worship. Summarize what the vows of baptism mean to you. Is baptism a spiritual milestone for you? In what ways is your life different because of your baptism?

baptism, believers experience the power that God used to raise Christ from the dead. Finally, for Paul, baptism served as a pledge of good conscience toward God. Including this pledge was a vital spiritual reinforcement as the first-century Christians faced constant persecution.

The Great Commission challenges us to go where we normally would not go and to face what we might not wish to face. It provokes us to become disciples in order to make disciples. It compels us to become the community of the baptized—those who have died to sin. Only Christ could make such demands of the early disciples and us, because he has all authority in heaven and earth. Jesus depends on the church to carry out his mission.

"Flying Solo"

Look again at Matthew 28:16-20 and at the various elements of the Great Commission: go to all; baptize them in the name of the Trinity; teach them all that Jesus taught. Your own baptism commissions you as a disciple; and this commandment is not presented as optional but as what any and all disciples do.

How well do you "fly solo"? Actually, even though you are asked to do your part in the Christian community, you are still part of a greater whole with whom you "fly." Do you feel the assurance that you are not alone in your discipleship?

"Flying Solo"

Several years ago, I worshiped with a congregation in which one of the famed Tuskegee Airmen, a member, introduced a blushing sixteen-year-old who had just completed her first solo flight in a single engine plane. Apparently, there is no other way for students to harness their courage and test their flying skills apart from flying solo.

In effect, Jesus' ascension forced the disciples to "fly solo." In the absence of Christ's bodily presence, the disciples had to depend on the Holy Spirit as their new Teacher. Now that Christ no longer walked the earth, the disciples had to continue his teachings. The ascension of Christ placed the responsibility of the Great Commission squarely on the shoulders of the growing body of Christ.

To the writer of Hebrews, Christ's ascension served as a sign of completion. The author presents the Ascension as the bridge between the earthly work of Jesus on the

that you are part of a greater whole? What does this mean to you as a Christian? as one who is sent into the world?

Jesus Christ Ascends to Heaven ■

Read Acts 1:1-11. Look at how Luke sets up his introduction to the Ascension (verses 1-5). Take time to discuss with one partner (or journal quietly) the events you would use to summarize Jesus' life and how you would introduce this final appearance of Jesus to the disciples. What would you include and why? What is the importance of what Luke includes?

The ascension of Christ was a sign of completion. What was completed? How do you think the ascension of Jesus Christ promotes participation in the Great Commission? Explain.

Bible 301 □

In Acts 1:8, Jesus was specific about where the disciples were to go. What is important about this specificity? Using a Bible atlas or the maps in your study Bible, locate these places. Look them up in a Bible dictionary for a more complete sense of what their

cross and his heavenly ministry as high priest. His ascension marks the completion of his atoning work. Christ ascended to heaven to offer himself as the final sacrifice for sin (Hebrews 9:24-26). Following that, Jesus sat down at the right hand of God—a place of honor and glory. There, Christ waits for his enemies to be made his footstool (Hebrews 10:11-14).

Jesus Christ Ascends to Heaven

We come now to the close of our study of Christ's resurrection, his appearances, and his ascension. Taken together, these events provide us with a wealth of inspiration for the present and hope for the future. God demonstrated his unprecedented power through the Resurrection. Through that singular event, God triumphed over sin and death. That victory provides us with the opportunity to receive salvation through faith in the risen Christ.

To confirm the reality of his resurrection, Christ appeared to his disciples during the forty-day period following his resurrection (Acts 1:3). In that time, he appeared first to Mary Magdalene and other women witnesses. He then revealed himself to the other disciples in various ways. To the disciples in Emmaus, Jesus revealed himself through the breaking of bread and fellowship. To the Eleven, he opened their minds to the meaning of Scripture. To Thomas he showed his wounds.

Christ appeared not only to verify the Resurrection but also to transfer the responsibility for his earthly ministry to the disciples. He bestowed upon them the Holy Spirit to empower them for ministry (Acts 1:6-8). He gave them authority to forgive sins and retain sins in his name. There could

significance is in this passage.

Jesus ascended into heaven, yet he promised to be with us always until the end of the age. How is this possible? In what ways do you encounter Christ today?

Close With Prayer

Ask for prayer requests from the group. After praying for specific requests, invite each member to reaffirm their vows of baptism and pledge to increase their involvement in carrying out the Great Commission in the upcoming week.

Pray the following as a group:

Almighty Lord, as baptized believers, we acknowledge that we belong to you. The seal of your Spirit has marked us as one of your children. Thank you for empowering us with your Holy Spirit. In humility and faith, we offer ourselves to you to carry out the words of the Great Commission. During this week, use our hands to touch people with your love. Use our mouths to speak your words. Use our feet to go where you are needed most. May you find us carrying out your Great Commission when you return. Amen.

be no wavering or uncertainties among his newly commissioned apostles. Consequently, the Lord dealt with Peter convincingly. With three pointed questions, Jesus restored his relationship with his most impetuous apostle.

Still, there was another person whom the Lord needed to propel his earthly ministry beyond the house of Israel. In dramatic fashion, the Lord appeared to Saul on the Damascus road two years later. The climatic event transformed the life of Saul, the greatest persecutor of Christ, into Paul, the greatest promoter of Christ. Under the inspiration of Christ, Paul went on to write nearly two-thirds of what became the New Testament.

We now await the second coming of Christ. Like the early disciples, Christians continue to receive the Holy Spirit's empowerment for Christian service. We receive our commands from the ascended Christ who sits on the right hand of the throne of Majesty. Our earthly ministry for Christ is not risk-free. Like Peter, some Christians continue to die as martyrs for the faith. Others grow old and die natural deaths. Nonetheless, we have reason to hope.

The Ascension story (Acts 1:1-11) ends with the disciples staring at Christ as he ascends to his heavenly throne of honor (1:9-11). As twenty-first-century Christians, we also are looking for the return of the risen Christ. We look with justified anticipation because of the words of Christ's angelic messengers, "This Jesus, who has been taken up from you into heaven, will come in the same way as you saw him go into heaven" (Acts 1:11b). Christ died, Christ is risen, Christ will come again.